Standing between the Worlds

You Just Can't Make This Stuff Up!

Standing between the Worlds

You Just Can't Make This Stuff Up!

In this tell-all book, Psychic Medium Krista Kaine
will delve into death and the afterlife,
and will reveal to you the intimate messages
directly from the world of Spirit.
As you read, remember:

You just can't make this stuff up!

Krista Kaine
Forward by Shanda Boone

© 2013 Krista Kaine

Published by: Krista Kaine

Editorial and production: Krista Kaine
Forward by: Shanda Boone

Additional Contribution by: Treva Ambrose and Kimberly Nelms

Additional production assistance by:
L'Vereese Britten, Jamie Broach and Archie Robbins

All rights reserved. This book may not be produced in whole or in part, or transmitted in any form or by any means electronic, mechanical, photocopying, recording, or other, without the written permission from the Author, except by a reviewer who may quote brief passages in a review.

Library of Congress Cataloging-in-Publication Data
Kaine, Krista ISBN: 10-1456422251

Standing Between the Worlds – You just can't make this stuff up!
In this tell-all book, Medium Krista Kaine will delve into death and the afterlife, and will reveal to you the intimate messages directly from the world of Spirit.

Printed in the U.S.A. by: Create Space, an Amazon Company

Copyright 2013 Krista Kaine
All rights reserved

ISBN: 1456422251
ISBN-13: 9781456422257
Library of Congress Control Number: 2010918094
CreateSpace Independent Publishing Platform
North Charleston, South Carolina

Dedication

This book is dedicated to some very *special children in Spirit whose stories are told and whose Spirit images are shared within the pages of this book: Hannah Ray Geneser, Misty Whitney Ambrose, and Zachary Shane Grimes. It is the beautiful Souls like theirs that bring such immense pleasure to my work as a medium. I thank you all for the gift of your presence during the readings with your families and for letting your loved ones know that you are never gone from them, but that you are truly . . . Eternal.*

A portion of all proceeds from the sale of this book will be donated to The Hannah Geneser Foundation for Child Safety. Thank you for supporting this beautiful and noble cause.

Acknowledgements

First, I would like to thank those of you who have allowed your intimate Spirit communications to be used in this book: Shanda, Jamie, Gretta and Dan; Dustin, Presley, Deborah, Michelle, Jodi, Leslie, Teresa, Kim; Treva and Brian. I thank you all for sharing such a deep and personal part of yourselves with my readers. Thank you for sharing your laughter, your tears, your heartbreak and your hope with those who have also experienced the loss of a loved one. You have no idea the healing that your story will provide to people who may be suffering in silence. You have given a tremendous and very precious gift to each and every person who picks up this book. Further, I thank you for entrusting me with something so personal and close to your heart.

To my family: Thank you all for your love and patience as I took on the project of writing this book. Thank you for your unselfish sacrifices and support of my work and the healing that it brings to others. Know that as my time has been spent with the families of other people, you have always been in my heart. You are my most precious gift of all!

I would also like to thank the people who pitched in to help transcribe the recordings of these readings for the purpose of this book. I am so grateful for the contribution of L'Vereese Britten, Jamie Broach and Archie Robbins: Thank you for investing your time, energy and heart into this worthy project.

Additional gratitude goes out to Jamie Geneser & Shanda Boone, Kimberly Nelms, and the Ambrose family for contributing the incredible photographs of your children in Spirit. They have given you an unforgettable gift by allowing you to capture their essence in pictures. I thank you immensely for sharing that gift with me and my readers. You can smile knowing that countless people will enjoy your photos.

Contents

Dedication   v
Acknowledgements   vii
Forward   xi
Introduction   xv

Chapter 1 – My Journey as a Medium   1

Chapter 2 – Gifts from Spirit   5

Chapter 3 – Understanding Death   9

Chapter 4 – Heaven, Hell and the Progression of the Soul   15

Chapter 5 – Spirit Speaks   25

Part II – The Readings: 33

Chapter 6 – Two to Three   35

Chapter 7 – Country Roads and Chocolate Chip Cookies   39

Chapter 8 – Cleaning up a Mess   41

Chapter 9 – I Love You to the Moon and Back!   45

Chapter 10 – Set a Place for Me at Thanksgiving   *63*

Chapter 11 – Someone has to talk about Charles   *81*

Chapter 12 – I've got the Dog!   *87*

Chapter 13 – Are You having Twins?   *97*

Chapter 14 – Don't give Your Power Away   *107*

Chapter 15 – 5x7 Sideways, on the Shelf   *123*

Chapter 16 – Show Me the Money!   *133*

Chapter 17 – How Much Money do You Need?   *149*

Chapter 18 – Bippity-Boppity-Boo!   *159*

Part III – Wrapping it up: *173*

Chapter 19 – Keeping the Relationship Alive   *175*

Chapter 20 – The Results   *183*

    Treva Ambrose   *184*

    Kimberly Nelms   *188*

Chapter 21 – The Cycle of Life   *193*

About the Author   *199*

Forward

I would like to propose a question to you, the reader, in hopes that you will be able to answer it from your heart by the end of this book. How does a parent survive the death of their child? How is it possible to get out of bed and face the day in the absence of your child's smiling face and heartwarming laughter? Where do you find comfort when you can no longer hold them in your arms and wrap your love around them?

Please let me introduce myself. My name is Shanda Boone and my husband is Jamie Geneser. Krista has spoken to our daughter on several occasions. Her name is Hannah Ray Geneser, and this world was blessed with her love and Spirit for four and a half years. She was our first born. Hannah brought us such incredible joy! She was funny and quirky, and quite happy being the center of attention. Best of all, she was compassionate well beyond her years. She knew how to love well . . . and that is how she won the hearts of so many. Hannah passed unexpectedly in an accident. However, that would be considered the "event," and it does not bear any weight in the discussion of Spirit connection. Letting go of the tragedy or circumstances of death is one of the hardest things to do, but it acts as an anchor which holds us in a place of anguish and despair. Krista has taught me that it is when we are in that place of despair that it is most difficult to feel a connection with our loved ones in Spirit. Our relationship with them will manifest from hope and the awareness that the bond we share can never be broken, not by death, nor fear, nor pain. I remember having a conversation with Krista about my reluctance to let go of the pain. *"The pain IS my connection with Hannah,"* I said. *"It is the way I am still able to express how much I love and miss her."*

Only recently have I discovered that my relationship with her can be so much more than that if I focus on the love instead of the pain. Love defined our relationship while she was in the physical, so why should pain define it now? By allowing myself to hold space for the pain to come and go as it pleases, I have opened doors to other possibilities. Some days I am paralyzed with sadness, but I know in my heart that tomorrow is a new day.

I remember when Hannah would have a bad day at daycare and get into trouble. She would be sent to bed early and we would discuss what she had done, while emphasizing that she could "try again tomorrow." That is some sound advice. We can *all* try again tomorrow. And that is what I do when I have a bad day.

I met Krista for the first time in March of 2012. It was suggested to me that I meet with her for a reading while she was visiting Des Moines. I was feeling discouraged about a reading I had earlier that year with a world-renowned medium. He was unable to connect with Hannah on an emotional or personal level. He definitely connected with her, but simply proving that she was present, and being able to capture her essence, are two completely different things. Krista was able to create a bridge that brought my daughter back to me and enabled me to hear her voice, see her movements, and feel her touch. For the hours she sat with my family, she was the embodiment of my daughter's love and laughter. She was as real to us as the daughters we tuck into bed every night . . . just in a different state of being. I left that night with a sense of reassurance. Although I truly believe, with all my heart, that Hannah is with me every day, it is all too easy to slip back into the feelings of solitude, emptiness, and desertion. That reading gave me hope.

The loss of Hannah, in the physical, has altered the course of my entire life. It has completely changed the person I am and the way in which I view the world, both the one we live in, and the one she does. The intensity of pain I have experienced is unparalleled on the emotional spectrum. And although it has been two and a half years since her death, I still live with the grief, which can sometimes be overwhelming, but now I live with it more comfortably. It is what I now accept as my reality, and with that acceptance comes a choice: I can let this experience change me for the better, or I can let it change me for the worse. What would Hannah wish for me? I will make her proud by showing her my strength and willingness to see the beauty in this life. I won't let her forget what my laugh sounds like. And I will ask her for guidance and forgiveness, and I will find the answers in my heart.

We, the living survivors of death, are not forsaken. We are watched over and guided in the direction of hope and healing. We hold the amazing power within us to create a fulfilling relationship with our loved ones in Spirit. That longing to hold them and feel their kisses will certainly consume us on some days, but the

Forward

ability to shift our thinking, if only for a brief while, can bring us much needed comfort and peace.

I would like to share a story with you. Recently my family and I traveled to Colorado to visit relatives. On the afternoon of the day before we left, the whole clan ventured to a park nearby. All of the little cousins were playing in a stream filled with boulders and beautiful cairns. One of them found a "magical" rock with a gold star painted on it. Pretty cool find. At the end of our venture, my husband, Jamie suggested that our daughter, Harper, throw the rock back in the stream and make a wish. After seeing the joy it brought Harper to wish for milkshake streams, every child just had to follow suit. My mother-in-law, Gretta thought she'd give it a whirl as well . . . so I thought I would too. I mean, really . . . who can pass up a wish? Since I have finally moved past wishing we could have Hannah back, and have set my wishes upon more realistic possibilities, I wished I could feel her around me more often, and that she would show me more signs, and that one day I may be able to actually see her or hear her voice. I wished with ALL my heart.

When we all returned from the stream, Gretta asked that all her grandchildren sit on the couch so she could get a picture. I grabbed my camera too. What a great photo opportunity! I snapped 3 photos. In one, and **only one**, there were three orbs . . . clear as day! I have never captured an orb in photos before that day. I know, without a doubt, that Hannah would never want to be left out of that picture. She granted me my wish. I am hopeful that I can continue to attain a more clear connection with Hannah. I want nothing more than to be able to communicate with her. Now that I know my heavy heart and deep sadness block that ability, I am trying my hardest to find a balance of grief and enlightenment.

Krista is one of the most amazing people I know, and she has become an essential thread in the net that catches me when I am falling. She has taught me so much. She reminds me where I come from, where we ALL come from, and where we will return to . . . with our loved ones, waiting with open arms. She also shows me, as you will see in the readings that follow, that Hannah is just as alive as she ever was in the physical, captivating hearts and taking center stage! I will never be able to thank her enough for bringing my daughter back to me.

I want to share with you a poem that I found shortly after Hannah passed that helps to shift my perspective when I lose sight of love's boundlessness.

Standing between the Worlds

I am standing upon the seashore.
A ship at my side spreads her white sails to the morning breeze
and starts for the blue ocean.
She is an object of beauty and strength,
and I stand and watch until at last she hangs
like a speck of white cloud
just where the sea and sky come down to mingle with each other.
Then someone at my side says,
"There she goes!"
Gone where?
Gone from my sight . . . that is all.
She is just as large in mast and hull and spar
as she was when she left my side
and just as able to bear her load of living freight
to the place of destination.
Her diminished size is in me, not in her.
And just at the moment
when someone at my side says,
"There she goes!"
there are other eyes watching her coming . . .
and other voices ready to take up the glad shout . . .
"Here she comes!"

- Henry Van Dyke

Introduction

I HAVE BEEN PSYCHICALLY ATTUNED FOR AS LONG as I remember, though for most of my life I tried to turn away from, hide, squash, or otherwise deny these gifts. It took me nearly forty years to finally release my fears, accept whom I was made to be, and fully step into that part of my Self.

Growing up with such tight constraints from the Christian Church, it was clearly understood that I was to be and act just as "normal" as the rest of the world. Though, the older I became and the more I began resisting the norm, the more inner struggles I experienced. For years I had used my gifts secretively. I worked as a Life Coach in many often-difficult areas of life, like relationships and personal empowerment; and although I allowed Spirit to lead me in my work, it was something that I had never revealed to anyone – not even my clients. I felt as if I was living in a spiritual closet . . . and I was dying to emerge!

Finally, I made the decision to allow Spirit to take hold of my life and do with it what It may. I had reached a point where I knew that I had to stop hoarding and hiding my gifts and step fully into service in the capacity that I was meant to serve. When I resisted my gifts, life had been one long, continuous struggle for me. But alas, following the path of my own Soul had finally become more important than the opinions, criticisms and judgments of others.

When I first began providing readings on a professional level, I was continuously amazed at how beautifully and fluidly Spirit spoke through me! To this very day – many, many years later, I am still consistently awestruck by so many of the messages given to me by Spirit! That's one of the greatest things about this work; it will always keep me humble to the spiritual Presence that is indeed . . . God.

After a few years of reading professionally, I had the notion that I would write a book – this book. I began to ask for permission from my clients to record their readings for the purpose of someday writing this book. I had originally set out on this endeavor in hopes of dispelling the negative connotations that many people often have about mediumship and other spiritual or mystical gifts. Unsure of when I would begin this process, I continued to record everything; every private reading, every group reading, and I even took written notes for the impromptu readings and messages that came to me so quickly that there was no room for preparation. I intuitively knew that there would be a day when I would give *the* reading – the *one* story so amazing, so awe-inspiring and heartwarming that I could finally say, "I have enough. It's time to write the book." That *one* reading – that larger-than-life innocent and amazing Soul finally came through for me in March of 2012. This little girl's name is Hannah Ray Geneser. And spending time with her, conveying her messages to the people with whom she shares so much love was the absolute pleasure of my life! I have connected with countless children, but Hannah is a Soul that is nearly indescribable . . . and a story that needed to be told.

It was not until I actually sat down to put the words on paper that I finally realized that my entire motivation for this book had completely changed. No longer did I care about convincing my extended family, distant friends, acquaintances, or anyone else on the planet that what I possess truly is a gift from God. Anyone who chooses to have judgment over what I do is simply exercising their own freedom to choose . . . and it is none of my concern. Now, I am writing this book to touch the hearts of its readers as I become the voice of Spirit, and to share some of the most the beautiful stories the world will ever know.

I now know that I am truly living my Soul's purpose and that through this work, I am helping to heal the hearts, the minds and the very lives of nearly everyone I encounter. This is what would be called, "good works." My work brings my heart inexplicable joy and a sense of peace and compassion that is unsurpassed by anything else I have ever known. Being a medium is not just what I do; it's who I am.

Thank you for taking this incredible journey with me. And remember:

You just can't make this stuff up!

Chapter 1
My Journey as a Medium

As a small child, approximately the age of three or four, I recall being terribly afraid of the dark, like many children. However, to me, the "Boogey Man" was very, very real. I saw him – or at least, what I thought was him. I saw somebody – the face of a man – up in the corner of my bedroom ceiling at night. This man never spoke to me; he just sort of hung there, watching over me. I could accurately describe him in great detail, which, of course, was excused by my parents to having a very vivid imagination. What I was not aware of until decades later is that this "Boogey Man" was a Spirit Guide; he was a protector for me.

You know the invisible friend that most children have? Well, to me, my invisible friend *was real*. Again, it was said that my "imagination had run wild," but even then, I knew my friend *was* indeed real. I spoke to her and she spoke to me; I heard her speaking, though not through my ears, more through my mind. She would advise me in times of trouble and she would tell me when something or someone was not quite right. I can remember times when making myself a snack; I would make something for her as well. That's how real she was to me. At the time, I had no idea that my invisible friend was, like the "Boogey Man," a Spirit Guide. When I was growing up, we were never taught anything about that, so I had no knowledge or point of reference for such a thing. Nevertheless, my *friend* stayed with me almost daily throughout the majority of my childhood.

Ever since I was about eight or nine years old, I recall having the ability to "*just know*" things, without any conscious knowledge from whence they came. From the end of our street, I could look at my mother's parked car in the driveway and accurately predict her mood; I would intuitively know if I or my stepbrother was in trouble. In my years of Jr. High School, my stepbrother (who was in high school at the time) would wait for me at the bus stop, simply for the opportunity to know in advance if he should be expecting a confrontation – if my mother knew of something he had done wrong.

I tried to share these "knowings" with my mother and my sister, but they always dismissed my accounts to an over-active imagination. It was not until I was a teenager that my mother gave any serious consideration to my gifts. I remember it well: I was fourteen years old and I had two friends spending the night with me. We waited for my parents to go to sleep so we could sneak out of the house and go to the convenience store to buy candy. My house was situated about midway between two 7-11 convenience stores; one at the intersection of Bee Ridge and Beneva Roads, and one at Bee Ridge and McIntosh Roads. These were the only places open 24 hours, therefore, they were our only options. We climbed out of my window shortly after midnight and began to head west down Bee Ridge Road, towards Beneva. After about fifty yards, I got a very bad "gut feeling" that had quickly turned into an overwhelming sense of fear and panic. I insisted we turn around and head to the other store. My two friends looked at me as if I were crazy. As they objected, I froze dead in my steps and refused to budge. It took some convincing, but finally my friends agreed and we changed course to go to the store east of my house, on McIntosh Road.

At some point during our late night rant, I knew we had been caught. I knew my mother had awakened and that she would be waiting up for us. Sure enough, my intuition was correct and when we approached my bedroom window to climb back in, my door was wide open . . . and there sat my mother.

Two days later, my mom showed me a newspaper story that had made front-page news. It read something like this: "Two Girls Abducted and Raped near Beneva and Bee Ridge Roads." The girls, who had also snuck out of their house, were picked up by a man as they left the 7-11. It happened around 12:30am . . . it could have easily been us!

After reading that article, I told my mom the story about how we were headed to that same store at the same time the other girls were picked up. That was the first time she ever acknowledged my gift of intuition. This turned out to be a very positive thing in my life; not only did I *never* sneak out of my house again, but my mother was finally listening to me about how I tend to *"just know"* things. At that point, I was able to tell her about many other instances where I knew or predicted moods, situations and outcomes. This *"knowing"* is not mediumship. It is psychism, which we will discuss more in the next chapter.

Somehow I knew that my intuition was related to or parallel to my "invisible friend" and the "Boogey Man" that I used to see in my room at night. Though my mother did begin to accept my psychic gifts, which she would only refer to as *"intuition"* or *"God talking,"* she did not want to hear anything about my seeing people or things that she could not see. In her mind, that was witchery, black magic or "Satan's work." She had no problems accepting my predictions and *knowingness* (as long as it wasn't called "Psychic"), but to communicate with Spirit was entirely too far off the grid for her. I was instructed – in no uncertain terms – to "shut that down," "turn it off," and "For God's sake, don't tell anybody!"

After the 7-11 incident, the use of my intuition became somewhat of a novelty in my home. My stepfather would show me the line-up for the dog races and upcoming football games, and ask me to pick the winners. Additionally, I became the finder of all lost things. If anything was ever lost or misplaced, I was sent to find it – and I usually did. Also, when Florida began a lottery, I was often asked to pick numbers for them. Although my family never won the lottery, nothing ever stayed missing for very long, and my stepdad did get quite lucky on the dog races and football pools.

Chapter 2
Gifts from Spirit

As I said in the previous chapter I had always been taught that being psychic or being a medium was "Devil's work." They were bad and ugly, and must come from a dark and dangerous place. According to my mother, people who claimed to be psychic or to communicate with the dead were either a hoax – there only to scam you out of your hard-earned money, or they were witches, Satan worshipers, or all of the above.

Growing up in an Evangelical Christian family, there was a lot of judgment around being or doing anything other than what you were taught to be and do. To be a Minister, you must be a married man with 2.5 perfect children and a pristine life. The Minister was anointed, part of a small "chosen few" who could access Jesus Christ, and was the go-between for God and the church's parishioners. It was perfectly acceptable for the Minister to lay hands on you and declare you healed. It was also commonplace for the Minister to prophesy over you while you knelt at the altar. Every talk, every sermon, every conversation was about how Jesus or God *"told"* the Minister something, how Jesus guided him and his family, and how he could "feel the presence" of Christ. Every Sunday morning, the Pastor would pray in tongues and declare his inseparable connection to Jesus and/or God. But that seemed to *only* be okay for the Minister and his family – surely not for someone who was not a permanent fixture in the church, who had not been baptized, or who was "living in sin." Please do not misunderstand my intent: I am by no means saying that our Minister did not have these gifts, in fact, I'm quite certain that he did. What I am saying is that we *ALL* have the same capacity for such gifts.

With my mother being so active in the church and with me being dragged there every Wednesday night, Sunday morning and Sunday night, it was imperative that I stuff my gifts away – that I lock them deep inside and not tell a Soul. This was not a direct instruction, rather it was implied. The alternative would be to confess to the church that Satan had a hold on me and that I was possessed by demons. Even that was not a viable option because it would not paint a pretty picture of my family for the members of the church. After all, the opinions of others were very, very important.

In an effort to please my mom and to escape the judgment of the general population, I turned away from my gifts. I pretended to be just as "normal" as everyone else . . . and I struggled! My entire adult life had become one continuous battle as to where I fit in, who I was, and what I would do with my life. Always having an innate desire to serve, I tried every service career imaginable; I waited tables, went into nursing, dental assisting, cleaning, sales, and a myriad of other service types of professions. All of these jobs yielded me the same result – I was dissatisfied and completely unfulfilled! The passion for whatever work I was doing had always quickly fizzled away and I was constantly left wanting more. I now know that this kept happening because I was not living my purpose. I was hiding my God-given gifts and trying to make myself fit into a place or position where I did not belong. I was trying to make myself something that I am not.

This all changed very rapidly in late 2001 when I was given express "permission" to finally be myself. My mother had passed away that September and one night she came to me in a dream. Her words to me that night changed the course of my entire life. I knew that she coming to me and giving me her guidance was a "green light" to go ahead and be myself. It was finally okay to stop hiding my light under a bushel and really, fully step into being "the Light of the world." This was the first step in a life-long quest for me; I wanted to know more, learn more, do more and be more. Beginning the very next morning, I quickly, steadily and methodically made changes, plans and concrete decisions about what I would do for the rest of my life.

I began by booking an appointment with a well-known and highly respected medium in Celebration, Fl., just a few hours away. As soon as I walked through her door, she looked right past me (and off a little to my left) and the very first words out of her mouth were, "Oh, your mother is here with us today." I was completely convinced that this woman was the real deal! She told me all of the things I had already known about myself, my history and my future. From that point forward, even until this very day, I have studied under and trained with some of the greatest psychic minds in the country. I wanted to sharpen my skills, fine-tune my gifts, and finally thoroughly understand who I am as a Spiritual Being.

I have learned many incredible things over the years, both in my studies as well as in the work itself. But perhaps the most important thing I learned came directly from the book that others had used against me in their efforts to stifle me. Most specifically, I studied the words written in red. I now realize that my work can indeed be found in Scripture: "The Gifts of The Holy Spirit." These gifts are: Wisdom, Knowledge, Prophecy, Discerning of Spirits, Healing, Speaking in Tongues and Discernment of Tongues. All of these words are written repeatedly throughout the Bible. Flip to a page – any page – and you will see at least one of the seven words written above. We will look at each of these gifts individually, and I'll give you a brief description:

- *Wisdom* – Deep Understanding.
  Wisdom is a sense of understanding things in a way that the brain itself cannot comprehend. Nobody can ever *teach* you wisdom. Wisdom comes only from a direct relationship with the Divine.
- *Knowledge* – Deep Knowing.
  Knowledge is the ability to simply know something, without having learned it or being taught about it. This is the deep knowingness that is often referred to as intuition.
- *Prophecy* – Prediction.
  To have prophecy is to have the ability to see (or otherwise know) something that will happen at a later time. This also can only be gained by a direct connection to God. When you are tuned in to ethereal energy – that cosmic connection, you can tap into the future to see what will, or what is slated to happen.
- *Discerning of Spirits* – Mediumship.
  Not unlike prophecy, this is also tapping into a dimension that exists parallel to ours. Our Souls are eternal and when we leave this body, we return to our Source. My son, Jason described it best when he had a Near Death Experience at the age of six. He said, "Heaven is not up there, Mommy," as he pointed toward the sky. "Heaven is right here," he added, as he motioned his arms in the air around him as if he were swimming. Jason went on to explain,

"Heaven is another dimension and anyone can access it whenever they want." Pretty amazing words from the mouth of a six-year-old!
- *Healing* – Realigning the Physical to or towards Renewal.
Perhaps the greatest example the Western World looks to as a healer is Jesus Christ. Jesus laid hands on the sick, and through Him, God healed. It's just that simple.
- *Speaking in Tongues* – Speaking in a Language not understood by, or filtered through the Brain.
This has also been called "the language of the Angels." If you can speak in a language that is understood by the heavens, you are speaking in tongues. Some may speak this language aloud during prayer, not even realizing what it is they're saying; while for others, it is simply a quiet, telepathic communication between the Spirit in you and the part of Spirit with whom you are speaking.
- *Discernment of Tongues* – Understanding Ethereal Language.
Simply put, this is the ability to have a two-way communication with Spirit. This is often a gift that is not recognized until much later in one's spiritual development. You can have the gift of speaking in tongues without the ability to understand what is being said back to you, but it does not work the other way around. You must first learn to speak the language before you can decipher it for yourself.

It truly baffles me to see that so many of today's Christians misunderstand and misconstrue the origin of these gifts, especially when Jesus referred to them time and again throughout the New Testament:
- *"All of these things I do, you will do, and more."*
- *"It is not I, but the Father* (Spirit that is God) *who works through • me."*
- *"I am merely a vessel, the Father doeth the work."*

This is no different for me or any other medium on the planet. None of us are personally responsible for the messages Spirit provides; we are simply acting as a vessel through which Spirit can speak. Our only part in it is that we have answered the call to serve in this capacity.

Chapter 3
Understanding Death

As a medium, I receive a myriad of questions surrounding death and dying on a daily basis. However, there is one question – a series of questions, actually – which I am asked all the time: "What happens when we die?" "Is there really such a place as heaven?" "Do we just go to sleep?" and "Do we get to see God?" I hope to answer all of these questions and more for you between the covers of this book. Death is perhaps the most misunderstood concept of all time. Though many try to explain it, most cannot even wrap their heads around the phenomenon that is death. In order to explain what death actually is and what happens when we die, I must first explain life and what happens when we are born.

Imagine, if you will, a river or stream. What is it . . . really? Where did it come from and where is it going? Rivers and streams are extensions of a larger body of water: its source. When a specific area of water branches out on its own, it becomes or forms a stream. This would be considered the "birth" of a stream. Every stream begins – and ends – with a larger body of water; it returns to its source. It is exactly the same concept with people; we are all extensions of Source, or God, if you will. Before we are even in the womb, we set our own individual course on the planet. Like the stream, we are creating our path; this would be our Soul. So, before we are even in-utero, we are One with our Source – God. When we emerge into being (upon conception), we are expressing our Soul, creating our "stream of life." A good way to look at this is to imagine a completed puzzle: before incarnating (coming into the physical), we are united with Spirit – we are "with God." Once we emerge into the physical, it's as if we have disassembled the puzzle and we are now that individual puzzle piece, whose mission it is to find our way back. It has been said many times, by many great spiritual authors and teachers that it is our mission to remember who we are, and to identify more with our spiritual nature than our physical. So, we begin as one small piece of a completed puzzle, and we end (when we are done with our physical body) by returning to the wholeness of that same completed puzzle. Simply put, when our body dies, we, not unlike the stream, once again return to Source . . . we go Home.

So, what then are we? Are we a Spirit? Are we a human? And what is the difference between a Spirit and a Soul? This is also tremendously misunderstood. Let's begin by looking at the various components of a person:

From the Miriam Webster Dictionary:
Spirit – An animating or vital principle held to give life to physical organisms.
Soul – A person's total self; an active or essential part.

This is a very accurate description. Simply put, Spirit is the life-giving property that is indeed *us*. In looking once again at a river or a stream, the water is to the stream as Spirit is to the person . . . it is the stuff from which we are made. Look once again at the definition of Spirit, but this time, pay close attention to these words: "Give life to physical." God truly is the *only* living thing in the universe – God is the "Vital Principle who gives life." This also is mentioned countless times throughout the Bible. The primary difference between the Truth of who we are and the teachings of most religions is that religion teaches us that we are human and that we must *invite* God into us. But the Truth is that without God dwelling within us, our human body cannot ever exist.

The Soul, as the "essential part" of us is how Spirit expresses Itself. In the example of the stream, the Soul would be our unique path. Therefore, we all share the same essence; we are all made from the same "stuff," though we are individuals, based upon how Spirit wishes to express through us. We are each our own stream of Life. So many people throw the word "Soul" around, using it as if it were an organ geographically located somewhere within the chest cavity. But this is a very big and quite common misunderstanding. The Truth is that the body is a tangible noun, Spirit is an intangible noun, and Soul is a verb. In the Introduction of this book, I spoke of Hannah Geneser and many others saying that I "connected with their Souls." However, that is not to discount any one of them as Spirit, because their unique expression *is* the Soul that Spirit chooses to express. You see, when the Spirit (of God) leaves the body, the body ceases to sustain. (Remember the definition of Spirit.) However, the Soul still exists because it is Spirit that has returned to Source.

When I connect with someone who has passed, I am connecting with their individual expression of Spirit (which is their Soul), via the Spirit that is alive within me. Spirit is life-force energy. Everything that is or was alive *is* Spirit. Just because the body wears out, does not mean that the Spirit has died. Life is eternal; there is no beginning, no ending . . . ever!

As a medium, I am simply connecting with, tapping into, or channeling the connection that already exists between us, though I may have never known them in life. The only reason there is a connection is because we are *all* pieces of God. It is as if we are each cogs in the mechanism of life that we call "Spirit." In machinery, it is the cogs which make the machine work, while without the machine; there is no need for the cogs. Our Souls are the individual cogs *because* each and every cog has its own purpose or position. They are strategically placed pieces of a larger device, just as in a puzzle, where each piece – as well as its placement – is integral to the completion (purpose) of the whole. We, as Souls, are also strategically placed pieces which carry out the function of God expressing Itself (making this thing called *Life* actually happen). Without God, there is no Life for us, while without us; there is no need for God. Without the puzzle, there is no need for the pieces; while without the pieces, there is no puzzle. Spirit and Soul are reliant upon each other; they are intertwined and you cannot have one without the other.

Remember that our Soul, as an individual expression of God, is how we differentiate ourselves, one from another. When I am connecting with someone who has passed, it is no different than having a face-to-face conversation with that person – personality and all. Many people would ask why their loved one was so lively or funny during their reading, why they (through me) behaved just as they did in life. The answer to that can be found in the Soul. If someone had a great sense of humor in life, they will express that in a reading as well; after all, it is *still who they are*. That great sense of humor was not something that happened by accident; it is one of the components that he or she had been given for the purpose of carrying out their mission, expressing their Soul. I have had many people in Spirit come through and either curse like a sailor or laugh like a joker . . . and I even had one ask for a stiff drink! This is a tremendous confirmation for my clients that I am indeed connecting with their loved ones. When Uncle Charlie comes through in a reading and shows me that he's fishing and wearing rubber waders, he is showing me what he loved to do in life. With that, my client can know for certain that I am indeed connecting with Uncle Charlie.

Let's look at this another way: If God is the only living force in the universe (which is true), and if our Soul is simply the manner in which God wishes to be expressed (which is also true), then speaking to someone in Spirit would look something like this: For one moment, put skin on God; let's make God a person – a man. This should not be a far reach for many of you with a religious upbringing. If I were to connect with Uncle Charlie, who has passed, it is essentially like walking up to God and saying, "Hey, do you remember when you played the part of Uncle Charlie? Well, can you slip back into that character again so we can chat with him?" It's kind of a humorous analogy, I know. However, the visual should help you to understand the connection that we all have to one another. We are all roles that God is playing . . . simultaneously!

At this point, you may ask, "What about the body?" This is perhaps the easiest part to answer. I'm sure you've heard the phrase, "I am a Spirit, I have a Soul and I live in a body." This has been an often-used phrase throughout my lifetime, most specifically within the Christian Church where I grew up. The body, which is animated (brought to life) by Spirit, is merely a vessel – a container, if you will. Let us look at this in another light: Imagine I am standing at the base of a waterfall, placing cups into the flow of water. The water is the substance that is contained within the cup, while the cup is what houses the water. Right? Let's revisit the parts of speech again and say this in another way: The water (as a noun) is what fills the cup (also a noun), while the waterfall itself is the verb; it is the Soul. It is exactly the same with our bodies and Spirit. Try to see the ever-flowing water as Spirit – the Spirit of God. Now, see the cups as the human bodies of people and animals; you, your father, your mother, your brother and sister; your neighbors, your friends, your dog and cat, everyone and everything that has ever existed on the planet. Spirit is the Source from which we are all made. When our bodies fail, the Spirit still remains, just as if the cup were to break; the water still exists . . . except now, it is free!

Need more scientific proof that we are not our body? Ask any physician or well-qualified nurse about a comatose patient. Can they hear you when you speak to them? Are they aware of your presence with them? Are they also aware when you are touching them? Can you pinch or poke them without them feeling or having any awareness of physical pain? It is my experience that at least ninety percent of these experts will answer a resounding "Yes" to all of the above questions. Let's look at this a little deeper: If what you really are is your body, then when you are in a comatose state, which is described in the dictionary as *"a profound state of unconsciousness,"* then you would hear nothing, feel nothing, and know nothing of what is going on with you or around you. After all, the definition of conscious is: *"aware of something (such as a fact or feeling); knowing that something exists or is happening."* Therefore, the brain (which we are grouping together with the body for this demonstration) by legal definition, has zero ability to know or feel anything while in a state of coma; hence it has to be a larger part of you that has such awareness. Knowing this, it comes as no surprise to me when someone in Spirit tells me, "I left my body" or "I wasn't in there." This is something I hear all the time with people who were comatose before passing or whose body suffered significant trauma prior to passing.

Most people realize that there is no physical in the Spirit world. However, as you read through the communications within this book, you will often hear me say things like, "They are showing me their head," "I see them with a drink," or "I see he wore a mustache." You may now be wondering: If there is no physical in the world of Spirit, how then can Spirit show me something physical? That's a great question! The answer is quite simple. Remembering that Spirit is made up of energy – as are all things physical and non-physical, you can easily understand that the energy that is now free to express itself can manipulate that force in whatever way it chooses. In other words, the Spirit energy can take many forms; it can bundle or compress itself into any shape, size, or color. When Spirit communicates to those of us still in the physical, it has to speak in a way that can be recognized and understood by the person with which they are communicating. Simply put, if you were sitting with me in a reading and I was connecting with your mother, whom (in life) had long, dark hair and was fifty pounds overweight, she would never be able to convince you of her presence if I said, "Yes, I see your mother. She is a beautiful stream of brilliant white light." When the individual Souls of Spirit commune with one another, they do so energetically, with no need for images. But when they are communicating with those of us still in the physical, they have to do so in a way that you will understand and can accept.

So, yes, it is true that we are Spirit, we have Souls (purpose of expression), and we live in bodies. Our Spirit is not *ours* at all. We are none other than the *Spirit of Life, Itself* – the Spirit of God. The core of *what* we are is merely an extension of that Spirit, an extension of God. The truth of *who* we are is the individual expression of Spirit, our Soul. And while we are here on Earth, we are housed or contained within these physical bodies, though the *physicality* of our "life" is in no way relevant to our **ultimate destiny**, for it is our *intention* to return to our Source.

Chapter 4
Heaven, Hell and the Progression of the Soul

THERE IS NO LITERAL OR GEOGRAPHICAL *PLACE* of heaven or hell; it is more a state of being, whether you are still in the physical world, or in Spirit. When we are remembering *who* and *what* we are, and when we are allowing that part of ourselves to lead us in this physical world, while in these physical bodies; life flows easily and effortlessly, just like the rivers and the streams, and the oceans that surround us. That, my friend, is heaven on earth! Simply put, when we live in the awareness that we are *none other than* the living, breathing, walking, talking Spirit of God, and when we are living obediently to God, by following our heart's desire, we are then expressing our purpose – our own unique Soul; and we are living in harmony with Life (God) . . . and that is heaven! Conversely, when we identify ourselves from the physicality of life; when we are so disconnected from the awareness of our true Source, from the presence of God within; when we begin to *believe* that we are this person, this persona that we have created; we are trying to disconnect from God, cutting off our own harmonious flow and disallowing our own inherent birthright of the proverbial "Kingdom of Heaven," thus we get to experience hell!

Since we are on the subject of heaven and hell, I feel that there is something which must be brought to light. As a medium, I have heard many eerie and farfetched stories of people who claimed to have connected with the "dark side." Personally, I have never had such an encounter, nor do I believe that such darkness exists. I do, however, believe in evil as being something created in the mind of the thinker. Let us now talk about heaven and hell, as it relates to the "other side." I will say it again: There are no such *geographical places* as heaven or hell. Heaven and hell are all a matter of experience, based upon each individual Soul. A geographical hell is absolutely non-existent! However, a level of progression does exist on the "other side." Since Spirit is eternal, the Soul is also eternal and has its own purpose. The death of the body does not void or erase the Soul's mission. The Soul is still focused on its own evolutionary progression and intent of learning what it came here to learn in the first place. Death does not undo any of that. So, as we move out of our physical bodies and merge with the dimension of Spirit, we are still forward-focused and evolving. There is still work to be done and lessons to learn. The level of progression that a Soul experiences is relative to their level of consciousness (knowing who and what they are), prior to leaving the physical world, as well their progression during their "time" (experience) in the non-physical.

A Soul Purpose Astrologer friend of mine, Lenore Hamill explains it with the most simplistic analogy. Imagine we are going to school. When we are just starting out in the school system, we begin with kindergarten. As we go through the processes of learning and evolving beyond the kindergarten level, we are ready for bigger and better opportunities and challenges. We then move up to the first grade, the second grade and so on . . . until we have a Master's Degree. The same is true in Spirit. For example, when I connect with someone who *recently* passed due to suicide, they appear to me as very broken and weak. I can see the pain they had when they made the decision to take their life, though they no longer possess or identify with that pain. The longer they are in Spirit, the more they evolve and the better they appear to me. It's similar to the understanding that "time heals all." An example of this would be that someone here on earth may have suffered a physical injury and the scar is the proof of that injury. However, after some time passes, the scar begins to heal and becomes less and less noticeable, until it is eventually non-evident altogether. I am not saying that a suicide victim is in a different *place* than the Nobel Peace Prize winner, Archbishops, or even the Buddha; they are simply in a lower or lessor state of *being* – they are still in kindergarten or first grade. Just as it is while on earth, a Soul learns and evolves through its experiences and relationships with others. They, like us, must still progress and learn to exist at the level of "heaven." That is exactly why we are here. Remember, it is part of our mission to learn to identify more with Spirit than with the physicality of our being.

Another question I am often asked is: "Does everyone go to the same place when they pass away?" The answer to that is yes . . . and no. All Souls exist in the ethereal realm – the *dimension* of Spirit, which is what many refer to as the "*place*." However, they also still have their own agenda and must continue to learn and grow through the progression and towards the fulfillment of that agenda. The difference in the agendas from physical to non-physical is that in the physical world, most agendas are ego-driven, while in the world of Spirit, the agenda is purely spiritual.

The one thing that you can be absolutely certain about when a person leaves their body is that in that very moment – that tiny, incremental fraction of time, they instantly begin to evolve . . . and they *know*. They know that the day-to-day dealings in their life on earth were not nearly as important as they had thought. They instantly have a keen awareness of the existence of Spirit, because there is no longer a physical body with which to identify. It is like waking up from a long, deep sleep . . . and being shocked from the realization that you've been dreaming all the while. When I connect with someone who has passed away, it is evident from the first interaction that they have indeed already made a tremendous progression, compared to when they were in the physical world. An example of this would be someone who did not treat others well in life, though they never found it necessary to apologize or seek forgiveness. The most sincere apology is almost always the very first thing that is relayed to their loved ones. Another example would be someone who committed suicide, but then found peace and joy when they crossed. This is due to the fact that the death of the body and re-emergence with Spirit has immediately created an enormous evolution. That being said, their work still is not done; they still must continue to learn and grow and evolve. I have connected with Pastors, doctors, junkies, suicide victims, rapist and the whole gamut of levels, from one end of the spectrum to the other. Each and every one of them, at some point – many points, actually – still has some work to do. That is one of the reasons they may not always be reachable to us. It is almost like knocking on their "door" to see if they can chat, only to find that they are currently "at school." They are in a process of learning so that they can progress to deeper levels of consciousness. Here is an example of this concept:

In early 2012, I was living in Mid-Tennessee and I remember noticing how I could not feel my mother's presence with me. This is something that has come and gone since she first passed away. This time, though, it felt different. It seemed to have lasted longer and, try as I may, I could not reach her! I knew (simply because of what I do) that she must be working on something. I had a dear friend of mine bring this up to me one day when she said, "I know you haven't felt your mom lately. Know that she's in a learning process and that she will be back when the time is right. I feel like she has some forgiveness work still to do." I knew my friend was completely accurate, and I had the notion that it had something to do with my stepdad, Jimmy.

Within just a couple of weeks of this conversation, I received a phone call from the police in my hometown. Jimmy had suffered sudden cardiac death. He was eventually resuscitated and sent to the hospital, where he had been in a coma for the last twenty-four hours. The moment I hung up the phone, I booked an airline ticket and began packing for a trip back to Florida. Once my suitcase was packed and the flight arrangements were made, I jumped in the shower. Instantly, I saw my mother. What a relief! While in the shower, she relayed this message to me:

Jimmy needs help to cross. He has a lot of fear about death, hell and purgatory. It must be all that Catholicism (she laughed). *He needs you, Krista. You need to be there with him and let him know that he has a choice; he can either stay or go. He's afraid of <u>where</u> he will go, so this won't be an easy task for you. You need to explain things to him, otherwise he will hold on way past the limits of his body. When he goes in for surgery, I will be there.* (Then, she showed me a vision: my son Kris, my daughter-in-law Keren and I standing at his bedside prior to surgery, though I had no conscious knowledge that he would undergo surgery. After all, not all heart attacks require surgery). *I'll make sure you can all feel me. You need to point out to them that what they feel is me. Let Jimmy know that I will be there with him and he will know that he has choice – he can stay or go. If he goes, I will be there to take him. If not, he's your responsibility . . . and good luck!* (She laughed once again).

After her message, she showed me photographs that she wanted me to bring to display in Jimmy's hospital room. I did not even know that these pictures were in my possession. So, after my shower, I asked her to show me where they were. She led me down to the cellar and straight to the boxes that contained those particular photographs.

Jimmy was in the hospital for ten days prior to his open-heart surgery. He was so weak and frail that he needed this time to be pumped full of steroids and other medications so that he would be strong enough to survive the surgery. During this time, I could not leave the hospital without Jimmy having some kind of physical or emotional crisis. During the few times I did leave, he went into respiratory arrest, tachycardia, and had episodes of hallucinations, thus necessitating my immediate return to the hospital. His fear of death had caused him to be an emotional vampire to my energy; he simply did not possess enough strength of his own to deal with his fears. I spoke with him on several occasions about what happens when we die, what the point of our existence is all about, and how his Soul is eternal. I reassured him that hell was not real and that he would indeed be with mom when he passes. I also told him about mom's message and that he would have a choice to stay or go. I'm not sure if it was the drugs or the fear, but I somehow felt that the message was not quite getting through.

On the day of dad's surgery, Kris, Keren and I were brought into the surgery holding unit. Dad looked petrified and overwhelmed with fear! As the anesthesiologist and two nurses were hooking up machines and IVs at the head of his bed, I stood on dad's right side and Kris and Keren stood at his feet (just as mom had shown me). A soft and graceful coolness swept across all of us in an unmistakable fashion. It was the most soothing, beautiful thing I had ever felt . . . and I feel Spirit all the time. Just then, I looked at Kris and Keren and asked, "Do you feel that? That's her. She's here." As soon as they both affirmed feeling her, my mom appeared at the head of my dad's bed, though I was the only one who actually saw her. Her presence was so strongly discernible that even the anesthesiologist looked over to us and asked, "Where?" I told my dad that she was with us and I reminded him once again that he would be able to choose. Once again, his fear was so strong that he barely acknowledged my words.

After dad's surgery, he shared the following story with me:
This was the scariest thing I've ever had to do! From the time I woke up at four o'clock this morning, and up until they put the mask over my face, I already had my mind made up. This is just too damn hard. I didn't want to do it anymore. I wanted to just give up, pack it in. But as soon as I went under, I knew that I was only asleep, not dead . . . and not even really alive either. I don't know how to explain it. It's like I was dreaming and the weird thing is that I knew it wasn't really a dream, even as it was happening. I felt like your mom was there with me, but I couldn't see her; I just felt like she was there. And I was ready – I was leaving – outta here! Then . . . I saw Jason

Standing between the Worlds

(Jason is my youngest son and he has always been my Jimmy's "little buddy"). *I saw Jason standing there with a fishing pole in his hands and he kept saying, 'Come on, Pa. Let's go fishing! And I had the sense that he needed me, that my work here wasn't done. I felt like my work now is not what it used to be or what I ever even thought it was; my work is just to be there for the kids, specifically your kids. So, I was like, 'What the hell. I'll stay here' . . . so here I am.*

The reason I shared this story with you is that it is pertinent to what I was saying about how once in Spirit, we still have work to do. My mother's forgiveness work in the time leading up to Jimmy's surgery was because she obviously still had some issues with him that she needed to clear up so that she could be there to receive him, should he have chosen to pass. Was my mom in "hell" while she was developing a deeper sense of forgiveness? No, though I'm quite certain that this experience has caused her to expand even more. It has brought her into a higher state of being, a deeper sense of purity, and it moved her even further into the *experience* of "heaven."

I'd like to finish this story by telling you what is going on with Jimmy today. This amazing man, who once could do anything, build or make anything and was completely independent, has spent the last year and a half living with me. He has lost over fifty pounds, is very thin and frail, and is often too weak or too tired to play with his grandkids. The height of his existence is when he drives to the gas station to buy his newspaper. Since his heart attack and subsequent surgery, Jimmy has had three more vascular surgeries; he has to have fluid removed from his chest every six to eight weeks; he has been diagnosed with lung cancer, needs a defibrillator pacemaker, and is continually visiting doctor's offices and having medical tests and procedures. He has spent the majority of this time camped out in front of the television and complaining about his various physical ailments. There is no real sense of joy in his life and the most movement he experiences in the course of a day is walking to and from the kitchen or walking through Wal-Mart, while leaning on a cart for support. Jimmy is on a myriad of medications, nebulizers and inhalers. Oftentimes he gets light-headed upon standing or moving too quickly and he spends nearly twenty-two hours a day in his bedroom, watching television. To Jimmy, this is "hell." So, mom was correct when she told me that he would "*hold on past the limits of his body.*"

Heaven, Hell And The Progression Of The Soul

So now we've spoken about one of the reasons a medium may not be able to connect with someone in Spirit. Another reason is relative to their current progression. Let me explain: I have a strict ethical policy that I will *not* connect with someone who is currently in a very low progression. As you read on, you'll understand why. By the same token, there are also mediums who are enticed by the idea of "dark mysticism." Those people will likely never connect with the more advanced, more evolved Spirit to which I am accustomed, nor are they likely to experience the amazing presence of angels. I'm sure you've heard the phrase, "You have to see it to believe it." I would submit to you that the opposite is true; if you do not believe in something, it cannot become a part of your experience. I do not believe in Satan, the devil, demons, aliens, reptilians, vampires, witches or fairies. In fact, I have such a strong disbelief in them that I would wager my last dime on the fact that they absolutely do not exist! Naturally, I have never encountered any of them. I do, however, believe that the more a person struggled in life with the understanding and acceptance of their true nature, the more work they will have to do once in Spirit. That's what makes children so easy to connect with, because they have a certain innocence about them, which affords them a much stronger awareness of "God within," thus having no (or a much lessor) sense of separation.

In all the years of being a medium and with the thousands that I have connected with in Spirit, there have only been two occasions when I have encountered a lower progressed Soul. One of these people was a young man who had *recently* committed suicide and still had a very long way to go in his progression. This may be what some would consider "hell." Within minutes of being in this young man's energy, I had to quickly pull myself away and cut off the communication altogether. It is not because he was "bad," "evil" or "demonic." He, along with the other person, whose story I have not told, simply felt negative; their energy was heavier. It really was no different than the energy you would feel sitting in a room with a depressed person; it's uncomfortable and weighty. No, they did not ever try to or threaten to hurt me. They did not try to scare me or "haunt" me. They simply had not yet progressed enough for me to feel good in their presence. I want to make sure you thoroughly understand that no suicide victim will carry that heavier, lower vibrational energy forever. Remember, it is their mission to progress, and progress, they will. Sometimes it takes death to show us where we have erred in life.

Perhaps this may be what some people are calling "demons." To me, this is complete and utter poppycock! As far as I'm concerned, the very idea of Satan and demons is just something that religion has created to scare people into handing over control of their lives – and I think it's an atrocity! To make matters worse, the media has gotten their hands on it in recent years and has extorted the concept of demons, simply to line the pockets of the television networks. That is a very crude and irrational judgment of these Souls and others like them!

I would like to share with you what I believe to be proof-positive of the accusations I've made about the television networks. When I went to Treva's house for her reading (which is outlined in Chapter 10), she told me after the reading that a popular television show had come to her home to investigate the "haunting" that was the presence of her daughter. With all of their high-tech equipment, they found nothing. They told her that it was too soon for her daughter to be visiting – not true, by the way – and they promised to return in a couple of months. Treva invited me to come back at that time and participate in the "hunt." Now, I had never watched any of those hyped-up shows prior to this day. After reading how I feel about them and the networks that exploit the myth, I'm sure you can understand why shows like that were never allowed in our home.

However, after talking to Treva and entertaining the idea of being present during the process, I decided that I would participate, even if only to prove to the show's "experts" that they were completely full of crap and that I, as a medium, can create an instant connection with those in Spirit, without the use of expensive bullshit devices. One evening there was what seemed to be a marathon of one show in particular. I will not name the show in this book, lest I be sued. I decided to watch as one episode after another showed horrified people who were supposedly attacked by demonic Spirits. Yeah, right! Naturally, there were never any witnesses to the attacks, only family members who claimed to have had similar encounters. Of course, these "experts" were never able to obtain any tangible proof of a haunting or presence of demonic Spirits. They were only able to decipher (because they are such experts) the strange noises coming through their expensive, high-tech equipment. Anyone could have done that and, if they are convincing enough, they could make you think you hear whatever they want you to hear.

After watching enough episodes to make me physically ill, I contacted a few of the people who had been featured on the programs. To each of them I made the same offer: I will drive or fly to wherever you are and I will make the connection to the Spirit that is "haunting" you. I will provide you a free reading, and then be on my way. In ***every*** case, I was told – regardless of how they made it seem on television – that the people from the show found nothing . . . zip, nil! I then sent an email to the show's network to make a request: Since in so many of your episodes, you are unable to prove or connect with the presence of Spirit, try bringing a medium along with you, even if only once. That way, the medium can establish the communication and you can compare the dialogue of the medium's communication with that of your computer equipment. The response that I received was completely expected, "This does not fit the format of our show, and it is not what the viewers want to see." Well, color me surprised! You mean to tell me that people *want* to believe in demons, hauntings, and things that go bump in the night? Of course they do!

I never heard back from Treva about returning to join the investigating team, and I was fairly sure I knew why. Nonetheless, a year later, I asked her what happened and why she never called. She explained that once she told the network that a reputable medium with a verifiable connection would be joining them, they declined the job and she never heard from them again. Go figure!

I have had many people ask to hire me to clear out demons and witches from their home. My answer to this question is always the same: "Who in your home watches horror movies and/or television shows about haunted houses and evil Spirits?" Every time . . . and I do mean every, single time, there is someone who does. As I said before, evil is in the mind of the thinker; hence the word "devil" is a derivative of "Do evil." One cannot do evil if they are not thinking evil. The "evil haunting" that exists in these homes can ***only*** be one of three things: thought form, created by the thinker (because they believe in it), Uncle Charlie coming for a visit, or the residual energy of a negative event, circumstance, or person. I could write a whole book about this subject alone, so it's time to move on. But at least I have addressed it for you and hopefully, given you some assurance that your loved ones in Spirit, regardless of what they were like in life, are not "burning in a fiery pit of hell" or being viciously attacked by demons.

In closing this chapter, I feel it is very important to ensure you once again that there is *always* peace in Spirit. Regardless of the current level of progression at any given time, those who pass are *always* in a much better space of peace, joy and understanding in Spirit than in life . . . but for some, it takes a lot longer to get there.

Chapter 5
Spirit Speaks

In explaining how Spirit communicates with those of us who are still in the physical, there are a few things to keep in mind. I will list them below and we will address each of them individually.

1. **The sixth sense is a heightened awareness of the other five.**
   Imagine we are putting together a five-hundred-piece jigsaw puzzle and I am handing you the pieces, one by one. I will hear something, see something, feel something (such as a physical symptom in my body), *know* something, or in some cases I will smell or taste something. This is your puzzle piece; I will tell you what I've gotten and I'll ask, "Do you understand?" If you don't, depending upon the importance of that specific communication, they may continue to give me the message again and again in various ways, until you do understand. Once you "get it," that is the validation for Spirit that you are making a connection. It's essentially as if you have answered a ringing telephone; the connection is established and the dialogue begins. From there, I will get more and more images, words, feelings, smells, etc., thus building upon the original piece and creating a clear picture that you can easily understand.
   - Symbols are very important in mediumship work. Not every medium will have the same meaning in the images or symbols they receive. Many may not ever see or sense the images that other mediums get. Most will receive their own symbols and it is just something that naturally evolves as they do this work. It's essentially the same as learning the alphabet; the more you practice, the more you understand. Remember that the Spirit of those on the "Other Side" are the Spirit of God. Certainly, the all-being, all-knowing

God is intimately privy to the things that are in my conscious mind and the experiences that I have had in my life. So, the images and symbols are *specific to me*, just as they are to other mediums. To give you a better understanding, I will share with you a few of my favorite images and symbols.

- For me, when I see a bouquet of flowers, I know that there's a celebration. So I will ask Spirit for a month of the celebration. Once I receive that information, I will usually say something to my client along the lines of, "What is the birthday, anniversary, or celebration in the month of September?" Now, if the flowers are lavender in color, I know that the event is specific to a birthday or an anniversary. If I feel like I am handing the flowers to my client, then I know that it is the client's birthday or anniversary that's being acknowledged.
- When someone in Spirit is telling me that they did not particularly like a person that they or their loved one is speaking of, I will see an image of a fan. I will then say to my client, "Do you understand that she's not a fan of his?" Or I will say, "She's says she's not a fan!" Another favorite image of mine is that of a horse's behind. When I see that, I know that the person we are talking about is (in the opinion of the person in Spirit) a horse's ass.
- My symbol for drugs and alcohol is that my nose will itch. This is because the first time I ever connected with someone in Spirit who had a drug problem, their drug of choice was cocaine. If someone was a moderate drinker, I will see a bottle of Budweiser. The reason for this is that my stepdad was a daily, moderate drinker and his drink of choice was bottled Budweiser. My symbol for a heavy alcoholic is a glass of scotch on the rocks, because my natural father was an alcoholic and that was his preferred drink. All of this is further explained in the section that follows.

2. **Spirit speaks in a way that the *receiver* can understand.**
When receiving and giving messages to a client, the person who is coming through knows that I am acting as the intermediary, the medium. Therefore, the messages I receive will be in way that *I* can understand and then convey to my client. Suppose I am connecting with someone who only spoke French during his life, and I speak only English. He would speak to me in English, so that I can understand what he's saying. It is not

necessary that he knew English while in the physical, because he is now in a position where he knows whatever he needs to know.

In keeping with the symbolic examples in the previous section, I may see a glass of scotch on the rocks, then a horse's behind, followed by a fan. I may say something like, "I see him as a heavy drinker who was not a very nice man – a real horse's ass . . . and your mom is not a fan! Do you understand?" Allow me to give you a few more examples of this:

This example comes directly from a reading. The client's father, who is in Spirit, was trying to tell his sixty-four year old daughter that he was watching her when the neighbor taught her to ride a bike. The image he showed me was what *I* would understand to be a little girl's first bike – complete with a banana seat, though it was not at all what my client's bike actually looked like. He had to show me in a way that I would understand, since I was the one passing the message along to his daughter.

Here's a brief story that should summarize my point nicely: Not long ago I was having dinner with my friend, Kim. I was explaining to her how Spirit communicates. Just then, a song came on over the PA system. I forget the exact song, but I do remember that its lyrics kept reiterating ". . . what a mistake I've made." I used this attention-getting song to explain about Spirit speaking in a way that I can understand when I told her this: "Maybe one day I will be in a reading with someone and I will be given a glimpse or a brief memory of sitting here with you tonight. Then I will likely ask, 'Who has the name of Kim? Do you know a Kim?' If they cannot relate to a Kim, I will probably say something like, 'Well, I am hearing a song about making a mistake. Are you the one who is making the mistake?'"

3. **Spirit presents in a way that the loved one can understand.**
I realize this statement may at first seem contrary to the heading of the previous paragraph, however, both are true. My clients can easily discern the person we are connecting with by the way they present themselves and the messages they provide. An example of this would be someone I have connected with many times in reading for her granddaughter and once for her daughter. We will call this person, "Helen." When Helen comes through for

her granddaughter, she expresses the same soft, loving demeanor that her granddaughter remembers her as being. Yet, when Helen came through for her daughter, with whom she had a very difficult and trying relationship, she apologetically spoke of her harsh, cold, aloof behavior. The irony of this was that I was reading for a private group and Helen came through for her granddaughter, and immediately appeared again for her daughter! The vast difference in personality from Helen really surprised me when I was reading for her daughter. Although I consciously knew she was the same person, I could not place her as being so during the reading, simply because her demeanor was so different. Her energy was completely different with her daughter than it was with her granddaughter simply because their relationships were different.

4. **This is *your* message, not the Medium's.**
As a deliverer of messages from Spirit, it is not my job to interpret the meaning. That's why I will either ask things in the form of a question or I will make a statement, followed by, "Do you understand?" During a reading, I may see a boat or hear a song about a boat, and ask, "Did he have a boat?" Or I will say something like, "He's showing me a boat. Do you understand?" The man in Spirit may have never owned a boat; it's not for me to discern. Perhaps what he is trying to relay to me is that he saw his family toss his ashes into the ocean from the bow of a boat. As a medium, I honestly do not know what the image means *to you*, because it is not personal to me; it is personal *only* to you or to the person I'm connecting with in Spirit.

Many years ago, my brother asked about me during a reading with a psychic medium. Most specifically, his question was about my career. The reader told him that he saw me "surrounded by flowers in about a month." My brother left that reading scratching his head. He called me and said, "Well, according to this guy, you're going to be a florist, and it'll be within the next month. Either you've been keeping secrets from me, or this guy is whacked!" About a month later, on September 23rd, the anniversary of my mother's death, I was sitting at the kitchen table writing my first book, "From Victim to Valor" on my laptop. When I briefly looked up from the screen, I realized that I was indeed "surrounded by flowers." Directly in front of me were two dozen yellow roses from my ex-husband; to my left was one dozen yellow roses from my eldest son; to my right was a mixture of lilies I had bought the day before; and on the breakfast bar behind me was another dozen roses, bought by my stepfather. You see, ever since my mom's passing, buying me an arrangement of her favorite flowers has been kind of a tradition for the males in my family. So you see, the message to my brother did not have any significant meaning to him, though it certainly was an accurate answer to his question because at the time that he saw me (in his minds' eye), I was authoring a book. This image was also quite a pleasantry because the reader had channeled my mother, who wanted to show how she enjoyed our little tradition.

I was happy to see that the medium who read for my brother understood and honored the ethic of not trying to interpret the message. Had he tried to discern – and therefore explain the meaning in the message, he would have been putting himself and his own judgment into it. That is a huge "No-No!" This is the same ethic I use in my readings, and it ensures not only the virtue of the gift, but also the accuracy of the message. One of the things I say again and again is, "I don't know what this means. It's not my message." There are times when a client will look at me as if they are completely lost and have no idea what I'm saying. But in time, it all comes together and makes perfect sense. This usually happens within minutes or hours of their reading, though if the information I had given them was predictive in nature, they may not see the validity in the message until it comes to fruition.

The first time I read for Lindsay, I was connecting with her aunt in Spirit. Lindsay had asked her aunt a question about her children; I believe it was something along the lines of wanting to know if major life changes would adversely affect them. Upon hearing her question, I immediately saw a little boy holding a small, floppy-eared dog; it looked very much like a puppy. This image hardly seemed like an answer to Lindsay's question. However, as a medium, I know that it is only my job to "give what I get," regardless of whether or not it makes any sense to me. In fact, it is my responsibility to **not** run the information through my logical mind. So, I asked Lindsay if she had recently gotten a puppy and she said, "No." Then I asked if she was considering getting one. Again, her answer was, "No." Still, I continued to see this image of the little boy holding the small floppy-eared dog. Within seconds, I saw this boy looking out through a window, into the front yard, dog in hand. I told

Lindsay, "I'm sorry, but I just cannot let go of this dog; I have to give you that I see your son with a dog or a puppy. And I have to tell you that your son really loves this little dog! I mean, he *really* loves this dog!" Understandably, Lindsay thought I was completely out of my mind! She walked away from that reading scratching her head as to how I could be so accurate on so many things, but then take a sharp, left turn into nowheresville with this dog that she does not own and swears she never will.

A few weeks later, I received a call from Lindsay, who was laughing hysterically as she told me that she finally understood the message about the dog. I asked if she had gotten a dog since our reading. She said, "No" and proceeded to tell me that when she pulled into the driveway of her home after an all-too-frequent business trip, she saw her son standing in the window, eagerly watching her pull into the drive. . . he was holding his well-loved, floppy-eared, stuffed dog! Upon seeing him, she immediately remembered that it was his all-time favorite stuffed animal. Her son was waiting to see his mom, whom he had missed so very much. So, you see, I had no idea what the dog was about or how it could possibly relate to her question, though it was indeed the right answer for Lindsay and her family.

5. **Spirit does not always communicate the same.**
   To understand how effectively a person in Spirit communicates with those of us still in the physical, there are a few variables to keep in mind:
   - How much they have advanced (progressed) since returning to Source. When we leave our bodies, our work is not done; our Soul still must learn and grow and evolve. The more advanced a person in Spirit, the clearer their communications with us. It is also true that when a person has recently crossed over, it may be much more difficult for them to communicate with those of us still in the physical world, which is one of the reasons why many of them come only in dreams.
   - If there is someone else in Spirit helping them to communicate. Many times I will connect with someone who has been brought through by another, more advanced Soul. This is especially true of parents and children or grandparents and grandchildren. That nurturing instinct is still present when they are with the child or grandchild in Spirit. Interestingly enough,

it is often the child whom will bring through the adult, depending upon the age of the child.
- The importance of the message. Not everything they say is vital information; sometimes it's just small talk, just as they spoke with you when they were still in the physical. You may also experience the person in Spirit simply going through memories, jumping from one thing to another. Children in Spirit are often like that, just as they are in life. Sometimes our loved ones simply want to chit chat and share a little time with us. Other times, there is urgency or a great importance to their message. Just as in life, when someone really wants to get their point across, they will.

6. **Some things are meant to be a surprise.**
If you are anything like me, you want to know everything; what will happen, when, how and why. Unfortunately, this is not how it works. When a reader tells you of something that has not yet been made manifest in your life, it is based on *current path*. You could change your mind tomorrow and make a decision that puts you onto a different path. Additionally, if the prediction involves another person, they also may choose differently. Remember, one of the greatest gifts we have been given is that of free will. Every decision you make will set the path before you, either in the direction you are already heading, or in an entirely different direction. You get to choose. Yet, at the same time, if you knew the outcome of everything, you would not have any room for growth.

Part II
The Readings:

Now that I have laid the groundwork and explained how Spirit communicates, it is time to move on to some of the actual readings. This should help you to understand how (in a reading) a medium will get from point A to point B, as the picture unfolds.

The first several readings I will share with you were never recorded and I am repeating them based upon my notes and the memories of myself and my clients. The first reading I will share with you, *"Two to Three"* is probably the most important and mind-blowing message I have ever given or witnessed! And yes, even W*my* mind gets blown quite often. Due to the seriousness of the events that were revealed and to protect the identities of all involved, I have changed the names of the people.

As you read these stories, remember:

You just can't make this stuff up!

Chapter 6
Two to Three

In January of 2009, I reclined in my favorite chair to catch a brief nap before my kids got home from school. As I closed my eyes and began to relax, my mother in Spirit came to me. This was something she often did as I tried to sleep, for that's when my brain is most relaxed, making me more receptive to the communication. I told her "Not now" and asked her to visit later . . . though she persisted. Almost immediately, she brought Dylan through. Dylan is a young man I knew who had passed away in 2007, at the age of twenty-one. I was surprised to see him and his presence was enough to get my attention and take the message. I asked my eldest son to act as the "client" for the communication and through a series of questions and answers, here is the message:

I need you to give my mom a message. Brent (Dylan's eighteen year old brother) *is going to get in trouble with the law. He will be arrested for a violent crime, involving drugs. This will be happening soon . . . very soon. He is guilty and he will need to pay the price. Do not let my mom get in the way of this; she is to stay completely out of it! This is something Brent needs to go through and it's an opportunity for him to become a better person. He will be sentenced to prison for two-three years.*

At this point, I will interrupt the message to explain how I got "two to three years." Dylan was speaking to me the entire time, via telepathic communication. He spoke. I asked a question. He answered, just as in a conversation between any two people. When asked if Brent would go to jail, Dylan said, *"No . . . prison."* When asked how much time he would serve, Dylan switched his communication style and began to hold up fingers: first two, then three. I asked, "Two years? No, three years. Two? Nope, Three? Two or three? God, I hope it isn't twenty-three years!" But all I kept getting were his fingers; first two, then three. It seemed very clear that Brent would serve between two and three years. But remember that it is *not* my job to interpret. The message continued:

*So, Brent **will** go to prison and he will serve two to three years* (shown only with fingers). *The most important part of this message is that mom is **not** to be involved . . . no matter what! She has to accept that this is something Brent has to go through to get his life together. If he owns up to his responsibility and will man up to the challenge, this will change the entire course of his life for the better and he will be able to help others in the future.*

After receiving the message, I made the call to Tracy (Dylan & Brent's mother) and delivered the message from her son. Tracy was certain that I had indeed connected with Dylan, though she did not pay much heed to the prediction for Brent. I heard nothing more from her for about a month.

In late February or early March of that same year, Tracy called me. When I answered, the voice on the other end asked, "Hey, can you tell me about Dylan's message again?" My heart sank! This is one prophecy I did not want to see come to fruition. Oh, how I wish he had taken a different path and changed it for himself. I asked what Brent had done. Tracy said he was charged with three counts of robbery and/or attempted robbery with a firearm. First, he went to his drug dealer's house and tried to rob him for drugs. When that was unsuccessful, he walked to the nearest convenience store and held up a couple who were leaving the store. He pulled a gun on them and demanded cash. Of course, the cash was needed for drugs, so the *"violent crime involving drugs"* was 100% accurate.

I reminded Tracy that she was not to be involved and that this was something Brent needed to go through. Tracy refused to listen; her only concern was bailing Brent out of jail and helping him to compile a case of "temporary insanity." Tracy worked as Brent's middle-man between him and his public defender. Even though the attorney disagreed with the insanity claim, Tracy persisted for months, even going as far as writing letters to the judge. The more Tracy pushed, the more difficulty she encountered. Just a few weeks before Brent's plea hearing, where he had planned to plead "Not guilty, due to temporary insanity," Tracy was forcefully removed from Brent's life. Tracy was picked up for some warrants that she had to answer for in another county, where she spent the next few months in jail. I see this as a necessary Divine intervention.

With Tracy out of the picture, I remembered Brent's fate and intervened on his behalf. I told Brent about the message from his brother earlier that year and I promised to help him through the process of facing the music. No, this is not a typical role for a medium, but I had known this boy his whole life and I knew how important it was for his Soul to have this growth experience. Within days of taking him into my home, the State Attorney's office had turned Brent's case over to a private attorney, who agreed to represent him pro-bono. Miraculously, the charges were reduced to charges that did not carry the "Ten, Twenty, Life" rule that the original charges did. I went to Brent's sentencing hearing about a week later, where he pled guilty to the amended charges. Brent was sentenced to "two years in, three years out." Better stated: Two years in prison, followed by three years of probation.

You just can't make this stuff up!

Chapter 7
Country Roads and Chocolate Chip Cookies

I MET TERESA AT A GALLERY READING I was conducting in Mid-Tennessee while traveling in the summer of 2011. Teresa had taken a couple of my classes that summer and attended some prayer calls that I hosted via teleconference. I knew her as a client, though I did not know her well. She had lost two husbands, Randy and Jack, respectively. But up until the night of this reading, I had only ever connected with Jack.

I was back in Florida in September or October of 2011 and I had just crawled into bed after a very long day. I could feel that Spirit was all around me, though I was exhausted and all I wanted to do was sleep, so I tried to ignore them. As I tried to fall asleep, I heard many people (Spirit) speaking all around me. They were all talking all at once and it sounded like talk radio coming from an adjacent room. After two or three attempts (and promises to talk the next day), the voices stopped. Except that there was still one annoyingly persistent man in my room – his name is Randy. I had a set of decorative butterflies attached by fishing line that hung in the corner of my room. There was a small bead on the end of the line to make the butterflies hang straight. Randy kept swinging the butterflies, causing the bead to hit against the wall. As I laid in bed (whether my eyes were open or closed), I saw shadows of large maple leaves all over the walls and around the corners, giving me the sense that I was on a winding road in the dark. I knew that someone obviously needed a message . . . now! At that point, I didn't even know to whom to give the message, or what the message would be. Then, Randy activated one of my senses that I simply could not ignore: He gave me the aroma of the most delicious homemade chocolate chip cookies I had ever smelled! The scent was so strong, so powerful that you would swear someone was in my kitchen baking hundreds of chocolate chip cookies! I finally gave in and said aloud, "Okay. Whoever you are, I will make the call," though I still didn't know who I was supposed to call or what to say. I stood up and grabbed my phone. In that moment, I knew who to call and as soon as Teresa answered, I knew the message: *Hi Teresa, I have a very persistent man in Spirit here with me, who smells like fresh baked chocolate chip cookies. He is showing me huge maple leaves . . . and I don't think we even have maple trees in Florida. I get the sense that I'm on a winding country road and there's a canopy of maple trees. He wants me to tell you to slow down and pay attention. Something is going to cross your path and you need to pay attention so you can avoid it.*

Teresa informed me that she had just dropped off her first mother-in-law, Randy's mom, Trudy, who used to bake cookies for Randy all throughout the fall season; chocolate chip were his favorite! After dropping Trudy at her house, Teresa was on Long Hollow Pike, a long, winding country road, with a canopy of maple and other trees. Trudy and Teresa were at a Democratic function that was put together by Randy and Teresa's daughter, Brandi. She said that Randy's favorite song had played twice that night at the function and it made her think of him. Teresa thanked me for the message and quickly got off the phone.

The following day, Teresa called me to say that when we hung up the phone, she immediately slowed down to the point of irritating the person driving behind her. The car behind her passed and, within minutes, a car sped backwards out of a driveway and across Long Hollow Pike. If Teresa had not slowed down, she would have collided with that car, likely being T-boned. This would also be a good time to tell you that Randy was killed when their daughter, Brandi was just nine months old. He was killed in much the same way, while driving down a road a lot like Long Hollow Pike.

You just can't make this stuff up!

Chapter 8
Cleaning up a Mess

In the summer of 2012, I received the biggest shock of my life when I was visited by a man whose body was still alive! As a medium, I am privileged to experience some pretty surprising and miraculous stuff, but this was even a first for me . . . and I was completely blown away! Perhaps the most beautiful part of this story is that it reaffirms for you, the reader what I have said about the Spirit, the Soul and the body, and the fact that Life is eternal.

I had received a phone call from an old friend, Rich, telling me that his brother, Alan was in dire condition in the hospital. He had undergone a quadruple heart bypass and never recovered. It was not until sometime during or after the surgery that the doctors had realized that Alan's heart muscle itself was too weak to sustain life in his body. Alan was moved from the operating room to a quarantined sanitary unit, where his chest remained opened and he was in a coma and on life support. That was pretty much the extent of what I was told by my friend.

A few days later, I was visited by Alan while in the shower. In life, I had only met Alan once, years before, for a total of about five minutes. I really didn't know much about him except that he and Rich had experienced a lifetime of sibling rivalry and that he had a previous heart condition. Consciously, Alan did not even know that I'm a medium or that I had been or would be in contact with his brother to even give him a message . . . but the Soul knows everything!

When Alan appeared to me, he showed me several things: his body lying in the hospital room, his family watching him from a window in the wall, Richard standing over him saying "He's not in there," some papers in his office, a tattoo on each of his arms, and another tattoo on the lower leg of someone else. This looked like a woman's leg and he was trying to identify her so that his brother could differentiate this woman from the other women in his life. Here is the message that Alan relayed to me for his brother:

I do not want to be here anymore; I don't want to struggle or suffer anymore. I'm not talking about struggling to live through this episode; I'm talking about everyday life struggles. I have struggled and suffered for as long as I can remember. I have hurt almost everyone I know and I don't know how to undo it. I'm tired of the pain and the drama. I'm tired of hurting people. I'm tired of struggling and I don't want to be the bad guy anymore. I am shuffling things around (this felt like money) *to keep everything up in the air. But if this doesn't stop, I'm going to end up in bankruptcy again. I just don't want to do it anymore. Please tell everyone to stop praying for me to get better. I wouldn't be anyway, I would never be 'right' again. If I got through this, it would be the worst thing for me, so please just tell them to let me go. I slipped out when the pain was too much to bear.* (He was letting me feel the severity of the pain in his body).

Alan gave me the sense that he really struggled in his relationships and that he had more than two women with which he was involved. He continued:

Please tell my brother I'm sorry. I always tried to make him look like the bad guy, but it was all me. I acted like I was better than him, but really I never felt like I was as good as him; not to our parents, not to women, not in business and not even in day-to-day life. I was jealous. I was an arrogant, rotten bastard, plain and simple. I'd really like his forgiveness and I really need his help. I need him to go into my office and destroy some papers for me. (He had shown me emails or mail and I sensed that they were proof of his current affair or state of affairs, like financial stuff, maybe). *Richard will understand and he's the only one I can trust to do this. I don't want her to find out this way. I was a son of a bitch in life and I don't want to be that way in death. I don't want to hurt them again on my way out. She doesn't deserve this – none of them do. I will come back briefly so that everyone can say goodbye . . . but I won't stay; I've done too much damage. My whole life is a friggin' mess! Just please tell my brother that I'm sorry . . . I'm sorry for everything.* (He showed me that he would "go" after he was transported.)

When I delivered the message to Rich, he affirmed that Alan was married to one woman, living with another and very likely having an affair with a third. I'm not sure which of them had the tattoo on her leg; that was for him to figure out, not me. Rich also told me that while in the hospital in the days leading up to his surgery, his brother was quite insistent on leaving the hospital "just for a little bit."

Cleaning Up A Mess

He said he needed to take care of some things at his office. Rich felt this was about getting rid of or doing something with the papers in his office. He also affirmed that, yes, he did stand over his brother and proclaim "He's not in there."

A day or so after I delivered the message, Alan was transported to another hospital, where he would wait for a heart transplant. He came back into his body briefly . . . just long enough for his family to say goodbye. This is exactly what he told me he would do. Although Rich was able to confirm that everything Alan told me was the truth – down to the last detail, he also stated that someone else in the family had consulted a medium who claimed to have made contact with Alan and said that he did want to live and that he would certainly survive this.

On the night that Alan passed away, I was driving to a private group reading and I felt him pass right through my body. I intuitively knew that it was Alan and that he was letting me know that he had gone. To me, it felt like a small "thank you." I spoke to Rich the next day and he told me that Alan had passed. I was able to confirm the time as being the time that I felt him pass through me. Rich said that he did try to get into his brother's office, but that it was alarmed and locked, and no one knew where to find the key.

A week or so after Alan's death, the family began to sort through his belongings. Rich was in charge of handling the paperwork, which was indeed a mess, just as Alan said. Alan had been shifting money around, robbing from Peter to pay Paul and had left a huge mess – even to the extent of cancelling his life insurance policy. Perhaps this is what Alan wanted his brother to take care of, reinstating the policy. Rich never did find the letters, though he did find that within Alan's protected office was a locked shredding box that an outside company would pick up to destroy its contents. With all of these events and details coming to fruition just as Alan had said, I knew that the message between the brothers was more important than ever and that Alan had given his brother something he really needed for his own healing. He gave him an apology and forgiveness.

This story is vital to the understanding that we are *not* our bodies and that our Soul's existence is boundless, timeless, and cannot be confined.

You just can't make this stuff up!

Chapter 9

I Love You to the Moon and Back!

$\mathcal{B}$EGINNING WITH THIS READING, AND IN ALL of the readings that follow, please know that there was some content that had to be removed, simply due to space constraints. Originally, I had wanted to keep every word of the transcribed readings. However, once the transcriptions were completed, the book was nearly five-hundred pages, so I condensed them by removing a few lessor significant items from some of the readings, and unfortunately, there were some readings that were so extensive, they had to be removed from the book altogether. In all of these transcribed readings, the statements that are italicized are direct quotes from the person I am connecting with in Spirit . . . sometimes even spoken in their own voice.

In sharing the play-by-play of some of my readings, I would like to start with one of my favorite readings of all time, a four-year-old little girl named Hannah Ray Geneser. Her presence in this reading was so special, so moving that I later asked her mother, Shanda Boone to write the Forward for this book. I will never forget the first time I connected with this amazing child! Those in attendance are Hannah's parents, Shanda and Jamie, and her paternal grandparents, Dan and Gretta.

Krista: Before we get started I want to tell you how this has unfolded for me. I received an e-mail from Lenore one Saturday afternoon last month. The e-mail came in at 1:26 p.m. I had an appointment at two o'clock, so I was in the shower when the e-mail came in. While I was in the shower I kept seeing Moses and I thought to myself, "Moses, really?" Moses of all people! And I kept thinking, "Is this Moses or is this Noah? Moses . . . Noah . . . Moses . . . Noah." I thought this was really bizarre and then I saw little hands turning the pages of a storybook.

And I thought "Wow this is really weird . . . even for me!" I did not see the e-mail from Lenore until I was in my driveway, ready to leave. As soon as I saw the subject line of the e-mail, I saw Moses or Noah again. As I was driving to my appointment, I started doing the itsy-bitsy spider.
All answer: Wow! Wow! Oh yeah! Oh yes!
Krista: I could not stop doing the itsy-bitsy spider and I knew that it was her. Just like right now I'm doing it as I tell the story and I just can't stop. That's her; she is doing this through me. While I was at this appointment, I told my friend, "I have a little girl here with me and we have to do the itsy-bitsy spider." And I just continued to do it; I could not seem to stop. I told my friend, "I know this sounds strange but she's with Moses. I can't explain it, except that I could be confused and it could be Noah, because I am seeing a love of animals." (I saw a lamb and a bunny) She liked little animals correct?
All answer: Yeah! Yes! Oh yeah, she did.
Krista: I thought that was so amazing but I have to tell you that I could not shake her. She was in and out visiting with me for days. I just kept saying, "I need to call these people." She just kept showing up, and I was doing the itsy-bitsy spider again and again for days! [Laughing] On the second day, I saw her face and I said, "Oh my word!" I was trying to get her name and I said, "Shannon . . . Amanda . . . and I kept getting A's and N's but I wasn't getting the full name. I kept trying to figure this out, asking, "What is your name?" This was consistent for about two days; every time I turned around, there she is, there she is, and there she is. This is because she needed to come through to you. She has been so excited about seeing you. During the time that she was with me, I kept getting that it was something that happened to her. I kept asking, "What happened? What happened?" What I mean by "something happened" is that I knew this was not her being sick, but something that had happened to her. It's like she hit . . . [smacking my hands together] and I did not understand what this meant. After that, I saw – and I believe it was you [Looking at Shanda], I saw you holding her hand. Is that correct?
Shanda: Mmm-hmm [Crying]
Krista: [Speaking to Shanda] Did you bring something of hers with you tonight?
Shanda: Yes, I brought this of Hannah's. [She shows me something she brought with her]
Krista: What is her middle name?

Shanda: Ray

Krista: She liked books.

Shanda: Yes.

Krista: She liked to turn the pages.

Shanda: Yeah.

Krista: And she would like to tell you the story.

Shanda: Yeah. [Laughing]

Krista: So, she turns the pages and she tells you what the story says. What was with the stars? Did she have stars on her ceiling?

Gretta: No, but we would look out the window when we'd go to bed and look up at the stars.

Dan: She has stars in her bedroom here.

Gretta: Yeah, she does have stars in the bedroom.

Krista: When I was on my way here tonight, I would close my eyes and see little stars and I knew those were her stars. Did she not pronounce her R's correctly?

Shanda: No. [Laughing]

Krista: And was puppy (pronounced) "buppy?" What was puppy? It didn't sound right. I'm trying to get what it was. I don't know if this is a dog or if this is a rabbit. Did she have something with floppy ears?

Shanda: They had a rabbit at school that she loved, a bunny at school.

Krista: A bunny! Okay. Bunny, not buppy. [Laughing] And with floppy ears! Was she trying to learn to snap her fingers?

Gretta: [Speaking to Dan] You helped her.

Dan: I was teaching both of them. (Hannah and her sister, Harper)

Shanda: Yeah.

Dan: Harper can now, but . . . she couldn't.

Shanda: [Speaking to Jamie] You taught them too. He was teaching them to snap their fingers.

Gretta: Can you remember if Hannah could snap her fingers?

Dan: She couldn't but she tried.

Krista: She tried, right. Because I think this is what I'm doing here [Laughing and rubbing my fingers together] But it would be more like this? [Awkwardly rubbing fingers together]

Shanda: Yep. That would be it. [Laughing]

Krista: She rubbed the material too, she rubbed the fabric didn't she . . . together like that? [Rubbing fingers back and forth]
Shanda: Yes. She rubbed the material of her blanket, yes! She called it, "num-num."
Krista: Because I was doing that on the way here, except I was doing it with my left hand, and I thought, "Oh it must be fabric I'm rubbing." Is there a brother? Who is the baby?
Jamie: Sister.
Krista: Sister. She looks like you, Shanda, blonde.
Shanda: I don't think so, but people do say that. Yeah, blonde.
Jamie: Yeah. Mmm-hmm.
Krista: [Whispering to Hannah] I'm not going to do that [Laugh] She liked to twirl.
Jamie and Shanda: Mmm-hmm. Yeah. She did like to twirl.
Krista: Because I feel like I almost *need* to twirl, and I don't want to have to do that; she wants me to twirl. [Laughing] So I'm just trying to do it with my hand
Gretta: She did like to twirl.
Krista: Alright. She would look at her shoes. Did she have shoes she liked, and she would have to bend over and look at her shoes like that? [Demonstrating]
Shanda: Yeah.
Jamie: She had sparkly shoes.
Shanda: Yeah. She had princess shoes. Mmm-hmm
Krista: Did she have something with duckies? What are the duckies about? I don't know if it's something for rain . . . but it's here. It's here in this house. (We were in Dan and Gretta's home)
Dan: She has ducks upstairs in the bathtub.
Gretta: That's right; there are ducks in the bathroom upstairs.
Krista: Were you not really able to connect with her before when you went to the medium in New York? [Asking Shanda and Jamie]
Jamie: It was difficult.
Shanda: No, not really. It was odd; not a real personable thing; not a real connection.
Krista: Did she have a loose tooth?
Shanda: At one point, yes. When she was little she fell and it was loose.

I Love You To The Moon And Back!

Krista: Well, she's just showing me that she remembers that. She played in this room. [The room we were standing in]
[Everyone nods in agreement]
Krista: I just want to tell you what I'm feeling and you can tell me where this comes from. Which one of you has guilt around this?
Jamie: I do. [Crying]
Shanda: Him more than me. I do too, but him more.
Krista: This is going to seem really strange coming from me, so know that this is *not* from me; this is from her. It has to be this way because this is something you will recognize that she would do. Can you face me and uncross your legs for minute? [I sat on the couch next to Jamie] Now this is something that she has done to one of you before, so you'll recognize it from when she was here. She knows how you feel. She would touch your face [I scooted closer to Jamie and touched his face, as if to wipe his tears] *"It's okay daddy. It's okay daddy. Don't be sad."* Please don't blame yourself. This was not your fault. Listen, you need to know that when we come here, we have a purpose for being here. And not all of us are meant to be here forever.
[Very tearful emotional moment for everyone]
Krista: And I feel that this has caused a big problem with the two of you. [Jamie and Shanda] Did you almost divorce or did you separate or something?
Shanda: After her passing or before? There were issues between us before.
Krista: Oh, did she bring you closer then?
Shanda: Her being born did. We were about ready to break up.
Krista: Know that sometimes people are just here to bring other people together. Sometimes that's their only purpose for being. When you have children that never get to be born or who don't get stay very long, it's usually just to touch the heart of someone else.
Krista: [Turning my focus to Jamie] You've bottled this. And you're not yourself anymore. Do you understand this?
Jamie: Mmm-hmm [Tearful]
Krista: I can literally feel your heartbreak. She was here for the two of you, for you guys to learn to love without conditions, and to see each other through the eyes of love and not any other way. That was her purpose for being here. She was your first. Crazy joy, right? Just crazy joy!

[They nodded in agreement]
Krista: Where's your daughter? [Asking about Harper]
Jamie and Shanda: She's at home with a babysitter.
Krista: Do you know how very special your daughter is?
Jamie: Oh yeah.
Krista: There are big plans for her. She's amazing, just so you know. If Hannah had not been born, you would not have had the second one, right?
Jamie: Probably not, no.
Krista: What is your separation? Are you in separate rooms?
Jamie: I think we're in separate worlds right now. We're not in separate rooms but we're not really communicating right now. There's nothing wrong with us, I think it's just the way we're grieving.
Krista: [Speaking to Jamie] I feel that you're bottling everything away right now and disconnecting.
Krista: [Speaking to Shanda] And I feel that for you, it's become your only focus.
[Tearfully, they both nodded in agreement]
Krista: But if the two of you could just find that middle ground, you could go through this together. Shanda, you are in counseling; but Jamie, you're not. Is that correct?
[They both agree]
Krista: [Speaking to Jamie] Because you can't bear to talk about it.
Jamie: Right.
Krista: Right, because if you talk about it, then you have to feel it.
Jamie: Mmm-hmm.
Krista: [Speaking to Shanda] And you can't get beyond it. You always talk about it, and it's all you think about.
[Shanda nods in agreement]
Krista: Is her sister two? Or was she when this happened?
Jamie: Yeah, she was. She's three now.
Krista: Who is the lady with her?
Jamie and Shanda: Her name is Mary Pat. She is a longtime friend. She's at home with Harper.
Krista: Can you tell me what the association is with Hannah and balloons?

I Love You To The Moon And Back!

Shanda: [Tearful laughter] We had a birthday party for her after she left. We let balloons go with messages to her inside.
Krista: Well, know that she saw that because she's showing me the balloons. Did you have the yellow one? Because she showing me one yellow balloon.
Everyone: She likes yellow. Yeah she did like yellow.
Krista: So she's just showing me what she likes. [Laughing] Did she have a baby cradle for a doll? And she would put her dollies in it?
Everyone: Yes! She has one upstairs here. Yep. Yep.
Krista: Is there concern or consideration about moving?
Shanda: Yes. [Crying] Yes.
Krista: Because it's difficult to be there, and yet you think that if you leave, that you're leaving her.
Shanda: Yes. Yes.
Krista: I'm going to give you a scenario about your house; this doesn't have to be exact, but it's the energy of it: "I'm not going to look when I walked past this area." Does that make sense?
Shanda: Yes. [Everyone nods in agreement]
Krista: It's okay because she's not there; she's with you . . . all of you. Realize that she's showing me things in your home [Looking at Dan and Gretta] and she's playing here. Did she lie on this carpet? [Pointing to the ground at the throw rug I was standing on] And she colored right here.
Dan: [Sobbing] Mmm-hmm.
Krista: Her association is with you guys; it's not with a place. Okay?
[Very tearful moment, everyone nods in agreement]
Krista: Have you made a modification to the house since this happened?
Jamie: Mmm-hmm. Yes.
Shanda: And we're considering making more.
Krista: You can change everything about the place, but you can't change what happened. Do understand this? [Jamie and Shanda nod in agreement] And once you do, it just may take away from everything you loved about it. She is with you, not the place – she's with you.
[They agree]
Krista: [Speaking to Shanda] Have you not been able to feel her lately? You did at first, but now you don't, correct?

Shanda: Yes, I used to, but I don't anymore.

Krista: You're still taking medication . . . but not as much as you used to, right? I get that you were taking medication to sleep. But not anymore, right?

Shanda: Right. I used to take something to sleep, but not anymore.

Krista: Have you stopped having the dreams for a while?

Shanda: Right. But I did dream of her just recently.

Krista: Yes, but that was after you knew that I was coming here and we were going to connect with her, right?

Shanda: Yes, that's correct. It was after we knew you were coming.

Krista: She is leaving something here for you. What is she leaving? [I ask Hannah what it is she's leaving for her mom] I do need to tell you that one of the ways Spirit communicates with us is through our dreams. But it isn't a dream; they really are there. There are also other things that you can look for; metals of all kinds like pennies or nickels that you just find laying around, flickering lights, and electronics going berserk. So what is it that you're finding in your house?

Shanda: [Laughing] Pennies. Pennies. Right now I have found so many pennies and it just started.

Krista: Are you looking at the dates?

Shanda: I do. [Laughing]

Krista: And are you recognizing that the dates coincide with something specific to your life?

Shanda: Yes. I found one that was 1974, which is my birthdate. And just the other day I found one that was 1979, but I don't know what that means.

Krista: Well, in 1979 you would have been the same age as Hannah, correct?

Shanda: Yes! [Laughing] Yes, that's right; I would've been. Thank you for putting that together.

Krista: And are you putting the pennies in a special place?

Shanda: Yes.

Krista: So, realize that people do this and that's just to let you know that they're thinking of you, that they are right there with you. You have kept everything of hers, and it's just like it was, right?

Jamie: Mmm-hmm. Yep.

Krista: And you have concerns that if you move, those things aren't there anymore . . . like her room.

I Love You To The Moon And Back!

Shanda: It's hard to take those things down.
Krista: Did she have a Peter Rabbit book?
Shanda: [Laughing] Yes.
Krista: Just make sure you keep the Peter Rabbit book with you. She loved that book! (This was the book I was seeing the month before) It's not a problem for you to move, if you want. I already know the answer to this but I'm going to ask anyway: How do you plan on getting through this?
Shanda: Well, we have a baby on the way. People keep telling me they think it's a boy; it's boy energy, but it is a girl.
Krista: Congratulations. You were planning on moving or doing something different before the baby.
Shanda: We thought seriously about moving, but we decided to make modifications to our house – to her room, to make this space more comfortable and not full of just Hannah memories. All of the upstairs is a big problem. So I don't know if we're going to move or not. This just came up in the last couple of months, and that's when we started talking about doing these changes just to help me cope with being there.
Krista: Is there a bay window?
Jamie and Shanda: No, not a bay, no.
Krista: Was that one of the modifications you are looking at? Because I keep getting them.
Shanda: Windows, yes, but not bay windows. We were looking at windows, yes.
Krista: Is there anyone else you would like to come through at this time – any of you? Who had a stroke or something with the head?
Gretta: [Asking the group] Didn't Gus have a stroke?
Shanda: Yes, but he wasn't that close.
Krista: He doesn't have to be; they're all connected through you guys. Who is Gus?
Shanda: The minister who baptized Hannah. He was the one who married us. He died not too long ago.
Krista: Did he go after Hannah? And it was a stroke?
Shanda: Yes.
Krista: He knew you personally, didn't he?
Shanda: Yes.

Krista: You know how much she is loved – and not just here. There are so many with her. (Gus and Shanda's grandpa was with her) Who is associated with a waterfall? I keep getting a waterfall.
Jamie: We put a fountain in for her. We built a garden for her after she died.
Krista: I am seeing an unbelievable amount of people gathered. Is that her service?
Shanda and Jamie: Yes.
Krista: You said you held her hand after, correct?
Shanda: Mmm-hmm.
Krista: Know that she is showing me that. And did you put pink fingernail polish on her before?
Shanda: Yes, and she put it on mine too. This was the week before she died.
Krista: [To Shanda and Jamie] Did she walk in your shoes? Whose shoes did she try to put on?
Jamie and Shanda: [Laughing] Both, actually. Boots, all the time.
Krista: [Laughing] Oh my word! Well, she was just getting into this . . . [Placing my hands upon my hips and being sassy] And it was very matter-of-fact, wasn't it?
Jamie Shanda: Yes. [Laughing] Mmm-hmm.
Krista: And she was a princess! Did she shush the baby? Shhh [With a finger over my lips]
Everybody: [Laughing] She shushed her sister, yes.
Krista: She had big, beautiful eyes. Can I see a picture, please?
[Dan gets me a picture] So precious! And such a smarty-pants!
[Everyone laughs and agrees]
Krista: It was "spy door" wasn't it? "Spy door" the way she pronounced spider. [Doing the itsy-bitsy spider again]
[Everyone laughs and agrees]
Krista: I don't know which of you she did this to . . . Who did she do this to when she wanted you to look at her: [I placed both of my hands on Shanda's cheeks and directed her attention towards me]
Dan: [Laughing] It was me.
Shanda: Yes, it was him a lot. [Laughing] It was me too, but mostly Dan. She did that to all of us, but she did it a lot to her papa [Dan]
Gretta: Yeah, especially him.

Krista: [Speaking to Dan] It was funny because I wanted to do it to you, but I thought, "No, I can't do that to him!" [Everyone laughs]
You know that the world really did revolve around her . . . as it should.
[Everyone laughs and agrees]
Krista: What is in April?
Everyone: A lot, actually. There's a fundraiser for her foundation, we are going on a trip, safety awareness week for windows, it's Gretta's birthday.
Krista: Okay because I have purple flowers. It's "poor-pull, poor-pull flowahs." That's how she is saying it. And it has to be for you, Gretta. Was purple her favorite color?
Everyone: [Laughs and agrees] Yes, it was!
Krista: Is her handprint still hanging up?
Jamie: Yes.
Krista: The right-hand, correct?
Jamie and Shanda: Yes. In the bedroom, yeah.
Krista: Did she like Barney?
Everyone: No, we would not let her like Barney. I'm sure she would have though.
Krista: Well, what's with the purple? Why do I keep seeing purple?
Jamie and Shanda: She just loved purple, and Tinky-Winky was purple. [They all laugh] She liked Tinky-Winky and it was purple.
Shanda: It's a Teletubby . . . A purple Teletubby. It might look like Barney to you.
Krista: Is it a big fat stuffed thing?
Everyone: Yeah. Yeah, it is. [All laughing]
Krista: Okay, then that's it. [Laughing] Did it sing?
Everyone: [Laughing] Yes. Yeah, it did sing. And she did love Teletubbies. Yes, she did!
Krista: She could have taken over the world. You know that, right? Very strong personality . . . adorable! And who did she call "Mister?" Pronounced "Miss tour"
Shanda: That was somebody at her school . . . Mr. Joe. But yes, that's how she said it, "Miss tour."
Krista: Did she not like her hands to be dirty? Because I'm sitting here and I'm holding my hands, and it's like something's melting in them . . . and it's like I've got to get it off! Did you make her wash her hands a lot? [Directed to Dan]

Gretta: Always! Papa was always washing her hands. [Laughing] And it could've been M&Ms

Krista: Something like that, yeah. You know, she adored you, don't you? [Directed to Dan. Very tearful moment] It's like the sun rose and set on her. Was she the first grandchild? Or just special?

Dan: [Nodding in agreement] Yeah. Very special.

Krista: I feel like you've all gotten to say what you needed to say.

Dan: Yeah, when she was laying there.

Gretta: Oh, yeah . . . Oh yeah.

Shanda: Yeah, but not when she was coherent.

Dan: Yeah, when she was . . .

[He cannot finish speaking. Very emotional moment]

Krista: Did she go into a coma?

Dan: Yeah she was, basically.

Shanda: Yeah, she had a head injury.

Krista: And it was for several hours.

Dan: Yeah, nine hours.

Krista: Do you wonder if she heard you?

Shanda: I do. [Everyone nods in agreement] I think we all do.

Krista: Know that she did and here's something that's incredibly important for you to know: You felt like it was significant pain.

Shanda: Yeah. We worried about that. [Everyone nods in agreement]

Krista: I need to explain. [Not a psychic thing] And this is something I actually got from my son's brain surgeon. The first time I ever heard this was from him: When something is too much for us, we leave our bodies . . . and we watch. She's telling me that she left. So I know what she's meaning by that. I'm trying to see this room from the perspective that she had.

**Note to readers: I will not give the details of this experience in the book, but I described the room she was in and her family's position in that room.

Krista: I'm just showing you what she's showing me, so you know that she saw this scene from up here. [An elevated perspective from the ceiling] Because she was not "in there." There was no pain with her after that. I know that was a concern for you, and you need to know that there wasn't. Now she's just going back to turning pages in her book. It's as if she's saying, "Okay, let's move on." She used her left hand to turn the pages, didn't she?

Everyone: Yes. Yeah, she did. She held the book with her right hand and turned the pages with her left.

Krista: Is there a story about her?

Jamie: There've been several. There's a video.

Shanda: I've written stories and articles.

Jamie: Lots of news stories.

Krista: [Directed to Shanda] Your writing has been cathartic for you. Are you writing her letters? Is that what this is?

Shanda: Yes, in my Journal.

Krista: Did you read something at her service? Was it the one with the poetry?

Shanda: Yeah.

Krista: [Making square gestures with my fingers, as if to outline a picture] Do you have one that you framed?

Shanda: Are you doing this? [Mimicking my hand movements] There's a picture I have that she made – a finger painting of a bridge; and I wrote a poem about that painting.

Krista: Okay. [Feeling like she was telling me it was her bedtime] She rubbed her feet together like this when she would lie down, didn't she? And she had little Fred Flintstone feet.

Shanda: Yes! Yes, she did. Fred Flintstone feet . . . exactly!

Krista: And she wasn't the easiest child to put to sleep. [Laughing]

Everyone: [Laughing] No!

Krista: You smell her sometimes, don't you? [Directed toward Jamie]

Jamie: Yep.

Krista: Is there something hanging at her school for her?

Jamie and Shanda: They had an art show for her. They hung her art. All her art was displayed.

Krista: What did she like to have on her feet?

Jamie: Princess shoes.

Krista: No, that isn't it. This is different. Slippers. Were they fuzzy slippers? Character slippers or something? [She was showing me bedtime]

Shanda: Yeah. Bear slippers.
Krista: And she had the long nightgowns.
Dan: Long Princess nightgowns, right.
Krista: [Laughing] She was in charge around here, wasn't she? I'm feeling like she's telling me it's time to go to bed. [That's why she's showing me all of her bedtime stuff.]
Dan and Shanda: Yep.
Krista: And she was even in charge of the remote control.
Dan: Yep.
Krista: And she could turn it; she could turn it to what she wanted. And why do I feel like I'm clipping my fingernails? Did she do that?
Dan: I would always clip her fingernails . . . and toenails.
Krista: Do you guys have any specific questions? Or anything you'd like to say to her?
Shanda: I have a question. What does she do now? What does she do that she enjoys? I know there're no days or anything; But what does she do with herself that she enjoys? I know she's happy, but . . .
Krista: She twirls. [Laughing] She's showing me that she twirls. Let me explain this for you: She is free energy that can go anywhere, wherever she wants, at the speed of thought . . . and then she's there, and it's like she's twirling. She loved to twirl. Did you hold her finger while she twirled? [Directed to Dan] Who held her finger while she twirled? Was it you?
Dan: Yeah, sometimes.
Krista: Do you know who she would remind me of as an adult? Scarlett O'Hara. Just that beautiful, graceful, a little bit cocky kind of larger-than-life presence.
[Everyone laughs and agrees]
Krista: Did she have the storybook Little Bo Peep? Because I don't know what the association is with her and sheep. But I just continue to get sheep. Did she have a stuffed animal that was a sheep? I don't know what this is, but I get this so strong. [It was reminding me of Moses or Noah, just like the month before] Was there something in her mother goose thing that had a sheep in it? Or a little lamb?
Gretta: Didn't she have a little thing that said prayers – a little thing in her crib when she was really little? That was a lamb.

I Love You To The Moon And Back!

Shanda: Oh yeah, that lamb! Yeah! Yeah! That was when she was really little. My mom got it for her.
Gretta: Didn't it sing or something?
Shanda: Yeah it did, and it kind of went back and forth and sang Jesus loves me. [Everyone laughs]
Krista: Okay! Okay, now I get it. [Here is where the biblical characters came in] This was just so strong!
Shanda: It's like, those things don't even register, and all of a sudden she talks about it and then I remember. Yes, and I've had that near me lately.
Krista: How interesting is it that she keeps giving that to me? Because I kept seeing this sheep, but I thought it has to be Little Bo Peep. So know that she has seen you with that.
Krista: [I drop to my knees in front of Shanda] I see that you're better . . . you are better. What would Hannah have wanted for you?
Shanda: [Tearful whisper] Joy.
Krista: [Whispering] Yeah. Yeah.
Shanda: It's hard to do.
Krista: I know. I know. Are you spending less time in bed?
Shanda: Yes.
Krista: Okay, good. Did you lose a lot of weight at first?
Shanda: Yeah.
Krista: But you *are* doing better . . . You're doing better.
Shanda: [She wipes her tears and nods] Yeah.
Krista: Are you three months? [Pregnant]
Shanda: Yes, a little more than that.
Krista: [Still on my knees in front of Shanda and Jamie] Hannah touched everyone's lives and she was here for a purpose. And I know that *nothing* makes it easier, but I think there's a lot of healing that needs to happen between the two of you . . . forgiveness. Maybe that was the purpose of all of this. I'm not saying it to try to make it like she was never here, because I know better. But keep with the really great memories that you have because she's an amazing little girl. Just remember the joy that she brought to you guys.

[Tearful silence, they nod in agreement]

Krista: Any questions? Any questions for Hannah?
Gretta: She knows how much we miss her, right?
Krista: Yeah . . . Oh yeah.
Jamie: What does Hannah want for this family now?
Krista: Let me quote her, *"Happy evor aftor"* [Of course, this is her annunciation of "happily ever after"] Who sees the butterflies?
Jamie: Shanda does.
Krista: That's from her. Remember, Shanda, that only love and butterflies are free. Know that she is with all of you. Know that she sees you. She says you snore, Papa.
Dan: [He smiles a teary smile] I miss her very much.
Krista: [Beginning to feel like a small child. It's coming through in the way that I speak] *"I know. I know. I miss you too, Papa."*
Krista: She's blowing kisses to you. Who called her Hannah banana?
Dan: I did. I got it started.
Krista: Thank you, Hannah banana, for coming through and talking to your mommy and daddy and G-ma and Papa. They love you so much! She showed me something and this is something she would have done for you before. I don't know why, but she has seen you cry before [Speaking to Shanda. She nods in agreement]. She showed me that she is wiping your face saying *"Please don't cry, mommy."* When would she have done that to you?
Shanda: She's done it to me before and I've written about her compassion, because you could even just pretend to cry and she would be very concerned. But I believe what she's showing you is when my grandpa died.
Krista: And she wiped your face.
Shanda: Yes, it was when somebody died; I believe it was my grandpa. And I was crying and she came up to me and she wiped my tears and told me not to cry.
Krista: I would like to tell you something that I see for you. Recognize that we all have free will and I can only tell you what I see for you based on current path, okay? We can always choose otherwise. But what I see for you is a collection of children's storybooks . . . and Hannah is your main character.
Shanda: Oh, I don't have anything like that; I mean I'm not currently writing anything like that.

Krista: No I don't mean currently, but Hannah would be your main character, right?
Shanda: I'm sure.
Krista: I see this for you and I feel that this is not just any other storybook. I feel that this is about an Angel named Hannah that comes to visit. And I feel that it's so that children can understand. And I'm just going to give that to you because it would be very, very healing for you and for many, many people. And I know that you're a gifted writer, and this would be an amazing way to turn this into something really beautiful. Okay?
Shanda: [Crying and smiling] Okay. Thank you. Thank you so much.
Krista: You're welcome.

I thought the reading was over at this moment, but Hannah had something else in mind. Once again, I felt as if this little girl were coming into my body and physically controlling my gestures and actions. I knew this was something the entire family would recognize as I dropped to my knees, lifted my head as if I were looking up to the sky, and outstretched my arms as wide as they could go. Then, Hannah spoke: *"I love you this much! I love you to the Moon . . ."* Before she could finish, the four people in the room broke out into laughter, and simultaneously finished Hannah's sentence *". . . And back!"* This was something that was very special to this family; this was the way they said I love you. And darling little Hannah wanted to leave them with what is a very familiar and very special gesture.

You just can't make this stuff up!

Chapter 10
Set a Place for Me at Thanksgiving

THIS IS A READING THAT STARTED ALL on its own, before I was even prepared. As soon as I stepped into the home of Treva and her son, Brian, I knelt to the floor in the doorway. Treva sat on the sofa to my left and Brian joined me on the floor to my right. The moment he sat down, I felt a presence that seemed to be most strongly with Brian. Although I intuitively knew that Treva and Brian both needed to contact someone that day and that it was someone they could both relate to, this particular presence seemed to be more of a friend to Brian than anything. I felt this so strongly that I had actually mistaken it for a friend, rather than the presence that Treva was looking to connect with. I asked Brian if he had lost a friend in a car accident; "something with some kind of an impact." Brian responded, "Well, sort of . . ." and he and Treva looked at each other. Treva answered, "My daughter, Misty."

The reason I had seen Misty as a friend of Brian's is because they are only half brother and sister, and they were fairly close in age. I began to get information, which seemed to come in rapid-fire succession – as you'll see in just a moment, and I needed to quickly grab my recorder and get started. Misty was so excited to come through and tell her family all of the things she has seen since she left, that the information seems to go quickly from one image to another, one subject to another. In an effort to keep up with the strong, intense energy of Misty Ambrose, I began quickly pacing in a small area of the room. My eyes were intently focused upon Treva and Brian, still by the front door, and it seemed as though this is the way this particular presence would have interacted with them.

Krista: On the way here, I felt like you had lost a child. [Looking at Treva] When I was sitting here in the floor speaking to you, I felt like it was someone who was hit. I don't know if that means car accident, but it was like, "Boom!" [Smacking my hands together] It was some kind of an impact or something that took them. And I got that it was a really strong energy. [I walked backwards towards the fireplace, my eyes still upon Treva and Brian who were still sitting at the door] But when I stand over here . . . Why do I feel it so much more here?
Treva: We have all of her stuff there.
Krista: You have her stuff there? [I turned around and saw dozens of pictures set up in a memorial type fashion, adorning the entire fireplace area] Oh my God! Wow! I didn't even look at that. I just walked over here backwards. [Once again, I turned away from the fireplace] I don't want to see her, not with my eyes anyway. [I did not want any physical influences during this reading] Can we please turn the fan off? Is anyone getting cold?
[Brian and Treva both agreed that they were cold. They were each rubbing the outside of their arms to try to stay warm.]
Krista: That's her! Do you feel that? Do you feel how cool it is? Are your hairs standing up?
Brian: Yeah! [He holds up his arms to show me]

Krista: Look at my hairs; they're standing on end and I'm freezing to death. And the closer I come to this fireplace, the more I feel it. And you said her name was Misty? Why do I feel like her crossing was someone's fault?
Treva: Because it was.
Krista: It was. Okay. In what sense was that? [Still smacking my hands together]
Treva: Driving too fast.
Krista: Okay, so she was with a friend and this friend was driving. This would be the friend that was not good for her and you knew that.
Treva: [Crying] Yeah.
Krista: Was her head impacted?
Treva and Brian: [Both nodding and crying] Yeah. Yeah.
Krista: I didn't even get to do my opening thing because she is so strong. She has such a strong presence about her. She is so like *"I've got to talk. I've got to talk."* [Feeling very wobbly on my feet and beginning to lean] Was she thrown?
Treva: She was ejected.
Krista: Okay. Did she go through the window when she was ejected? Or through something?
Treva: She went through the side window.
Krista: The side window. Okay. Because it's like I'm standing here and I feel like I'm being thrown. This is your heartbreak that I felt on the way here. [Looking at Treva] You have never gotten over this, have you?
Treva: [Very emotional. No words, just agreement]
Krista: This happened within . . . [Holding up three fingers] Was it recent?
Brian: Mmm-hmm.
Krista: Okay. Is there an anniversary or something coming up with her? Anniversary, birthday or celebration. [Not really able to pinpoint it]
Brian: Something of her favorite.
Krista: Okay. What is that?
Brian: Halloween.
Krista: What is it you're doing for her? What is it you'll do for her at this time? Do you decorate specifically for her, or is there a specific decoration? Because she's telling me that there's something you're going to do and she's going to be there when you do it. And it feels like the way you decorate, or something along those lines. Tell me what this is.

Brian: We're going to roll the tree. [He is referring to decorating the tree that she hit with toilet paper]
Treva: [Crying] At the crash site.
Krista: You have already planned this. So know that in order for me to know what you are going to do, this is her watching you. She's here and she knows everything, and I feel like she spends a lot of time right here, in this area. [I pointed to a specific place in the room] And know that when she tells me what you are going to do, that is your way of knowing that she's saying: *"I'm watching, I'm listening, I know."* And I have to tell you, Treva, because I know that this has probably been the thing that has weighed on you the most is her pain. She wants you to know that it did not hurt. It's almost like an out of body experience. It's like that. She wants you to know it did not hurt. And the only thing that has hurt in all of this is watching you.
Treva: [Very emotional] Yeah.
Krista: Why is she telling me that she's free? Was she troubled? She had struggles in life. I feel like she had a sense of struggle or being stuck. But she wants you to know that she's free, okay?
Krista: [Shifting my attention to Brian] You are the one who doesn't talk about it, aren't you?
Brian: [Very emotional, he nods in agreement]
Krista: And you think that sweeping it under the rug will make it go away. You know better, but you still do it.
Brian: Mmm-hmm.
Krista: Were you guys pretty close in age? I don't know if this is when you guys were younger or if this was recent, but the reason I ask if you are close in age is because she tells me that . . . Well, how do I say this? I don't know if you were a real pain to her, or she was a real pain to you. Which was it?
Brian: [Laughing] I think it was both.
Krista: And was it only when you were younger, or was it even up until this point?
Brian: [Still laughing] All the way!
Krista: [Laughing] *"And that's just what we did."* That's what she says: *"That's just what we did. That's how we were."* But she always knew you loved her. You didn't even know how much you love her, did you . . . until she left?
Brian: [Crying] Right.

Krista: She does not want you to have guilt, she doesn't. I don't know what your last interactions were with her, but she does not want you to have guilt about it. She says, *"I've always loved you and I know you always loved me."* And she wants you to know that it's okay. And you talk to her. You pray and talk to her, don't you?

Brian: [Very emotional, nodding in agreement]

Krista: And this is something you probably don't even know, do you, mom? [Shifting my attention to Treva]

Treva: [Very emotional] No, I didn't.

Krista: Well, he does. And she's showing me that. [Returning my focus to Brian] That's when you finally let yourself release, that's when you let yourself cry, that's when you let yourself feel. So know that she's there with you when you do that and she said that she hears you. Which one of you was looking for a scholarship? Was she looking for scholarship, or were you looking for scholarship?

Brian: [Smiling] I kind of was; I was looking more towards business.

Krista: So what happened to that? Because I got that there was a scholarship, and it went away. Did you change your mind?

Brian: Yeah.

Krista: Because you haven't been right since she left. You stopped focusing on yourself.

Brian: Yeah, but I don't know what I want.

Krista: Why she telling me that you would be good at marketing?

Brian: Because I'm a good seller. [Laughing]

Krista: And you're friendly and people like you. When you said you didn't know what you wanted, she said, *"Well what about marketing?"* So I'm going to put that out there to you, and if you can refocus yourself, you can have whatever you want. You know this. In your heart, you know this.

Brian: Mmm-hmm.

Krista: Treva, what is it that you guys made? [Misty shows me her in the kitchen with Treva] Did you make cookies or cupcakes or something? You made something for a time that is coming up. I don't know if it's around Halloween, but it feels like something you bake, like a treat. But, it's about the two of you. What is it that you used to bring to her classroom?

Treva: Oh yeah, that would be cupcakes.

Krista: Were they for the holiday? Like holiday parties or something? At first I thought it was something that you were baking, but I think it's just something that's baked, like cupcakes or cookies or something.
Treva: Yeah, I would bring cupcakes.
Krista: Okay. Did you start grief counseling and not finish?
Treva: I went for a little bit.
Krista: Because you didn't think it was going to go away. You didn't think you were making progress. I don't know what it was, but she said you didn't finish the counseling.
Treva: The man didn't know what he was talking about. He just didn't know how we felt.
Krista: And he never could.
Treva: Right!
Krista: He could never know how you feel. Do you have her room still set up? Because she is showing me her room.
Treva: Yeah.
Krista: Can we go? Can we go to her room?
Treva: Yes we can. [She leads us to Misty's room]
Krista: I'm looking for a stuffed animal. Where are the rest of her stuffed animals?
Treva: We put them away.
Krista: There was a white one. I don't know if it's a unicorn, pony, bunny, or something like that. It feels older; like something she had when she was a lot younger. Do you know which one I'm talking about?
Treva: Mmm-hmm. Mmm-hmm.
Krista: How long has she been gone?
Treva: A little bit over three months.
Krista: Whose birthday did she miss? She tells me that she missed a birthday, and that it just wasn't the same without her there. Was that your birthday? [Directed towards Brian]
Brian and Treva: Mmm-hmm. Yeah.
Krista: I get the sense that you didn't even want a birthday; like you just didn't want anything to do with it.
Brian: [Emotional] Mmm-hmm.
Krista: Was she cremated?

Treva: [Shaking her head] No.
Krista: Okay, well I'm looking for some type of an urn, a vase, or something along those lines. [Using my hands to show them the size and shape of this object] She is showing me the shape of it and it's shaped like an urn. What is that? It's in this house. [We all begin to look around the room and Brian spots a large, urn-shaped vase] This is it! What is specific about this?
Treva: I had her flowers in there.
Krista: Okay, that explains it. Flowers from when she passed.
Treva: Mmm-hmm.
Krista: Okay. Please know that she was showing me that, and I knew it had something to do with her crossing. What does she have coming up and she wasn't able to do? It's like she had plans.
Treva: Oh yeah, she had plenty of plans!
Brian: [Laughing] High school.
Treva: Yeah, high school. (Misty passed just a few months before her freshman year of high school)
Krista: Can I ask you what her sign is? When was she born?
Treva: She's a Capricorn.
Krista: Oh, that explains it! Capricorns are loaded with plans! They have to do everything and they're very focused. They want everything and they have a plan to get to it. So she's telling me that she never got to keep her plans. She knows how proud you are of her, and I get the feeling that it wasn't always expressed.
Treva: [Very emotional, she agrees]
Krista: Know that she knows . . . and it's okay. It's okay. Of course she misses you guys, but it's okay. She is not hurting and she is free. And she is always, always with you.
Krista: [Directed to Treva] Did you spend a lot of time in bed after this happened?
Treva: [Crying] Mmm-hmm.
Krista: She is showing me this and it's almost like . . . I don't know if this is exact, or if it's just the energy of it, but it's almost like you didn't even want to take a shower or anything, or brush you hair or anything else. You just wanted to be in bed.
[Treva agrees]

Krista: She's saying, *"That's not how my mom is!"* That's just not you! Because usually you have a lot of things to do and you're just go, go, go. So know that she's here and she sees what you've been going through. Were there a lot of young people there at her services? Like people that you didn't even expect?
Treva: Yeah.
Krista: I get the sense that it was a lot more than you expected.
Treva: Yeah. Oh yeah.
Krista: Who spoke at her services? Who stood up and said something about her?
Treva: Her uncle. He did.
Krista: She's showing me her service. Who wrote something for her?
Brian: Her uncle.
Treva: My brother. [She hands me what was written for Misty]
Krista: Is he going to frame it? Or what's he going to do with it?
Brian: Put it away.
Treva: Probably put it away.
Krista: She would like to see it framed. [We all laugh] So know that she was there during the service. I get that a lot; there a lot of people who stick around for their services. She was surprised at how many people came. She would like to see her uncle's writing framed.
Krista: Is there another child? Who is this other child?
Treva: She's got two more sisters.
Krista: Younger. Who has a young child? [Holding up my hand to indicate the size of a small child]
Brian and Treva: Katie. Yeah, Katie.
Krista: Who is Katie?
Brian: Her favorite little niece.
Krista: Okay because it's like they were so close that I thought it was like a little sister. They were just that connected! So Misty is the aunt then, right?
Treva: Yes.
Krista: What is this child's name?
Treva: Cadence. (They call her Katie)
Krista: She just loves seeing Cadence bebop around. Is she loaded with energy?
Treva and Brian: Oh yeah! Mmm-hmm.
Krista: How old? Like this? [Holding five fingers up in the air]

Treva: Yeah. She's five.
Krista: Did this happen at night? I get the sense that it was evening, the end of the day.
Treva: Yeah. Yeah.
Krista: Do you have the ribbon?
Treva: [Nods in agreement]
Krista: I get the sense of a ribbon that goes into flowers or a ribbon that goes on the casket or something. What is the ribbon? She's showing me a ribbon.
Treva: [Emotional] I made the ribbons.
Krista: You made the ribbons, okay. And you still have them.
Treva: Some of them. Yeah.
Krista: So know that for her to tell me which stuffed animal to ask for, the shape of the vase, the ribbons; know that from the moment she left, she's been watching everything. Know that . . . because she has. I could not possibly know any of this unless she told me and she was there as it happened. She would love to see you [Directed to Treva] get some help with this, because she said you didn't finish the counseling. Because you're starting to do what he does. [Pointing to Brian] You're starting to bury it, aren't you? And just pretend you don't hurt?
Treva: [Very emotional, agrees]
Krista: Which one of her grandmothers would've done something like that? Just not addressed how they felt and just buried it? Because she says, *"Just like grandma would."* Is that *your* mother? [Directed to Treva]
Treva: Yes, my mama.
Brian: Yeah. Nanny.
Krista: This is interesting because she actually has a sense of excitement about all that she knows now. You are definitely on the right track [Speaking to Brian]. This is talking about your spiritual awareness: you are definitely on the right track! And she wants you to know that. She says it's not what we would have thought it was.
Brian: I get what you're going toward; it wasn't supposed to be her. It was supposed to be me. I've had many wrecks, many accidents, due to my judgment of speeding. I love to race.
Krista: Okay, so that would be your guilt that she talked about earlier. [I get the sense there's something more] Or part of it, maybe.
Brian: We were in an argument, so that's the guilt that I feel.

Krista: Okay. Did someone have a tattoo? Or was someone thinking about getting a tattoo?
[Brian and Treva both laugh aloud]
Brian: Mom and dad were thinking about getting one.
Krista: So, she's showing me the tattoo. And she loves that! Know that she is always, always with you. She has not left you. She misses you, but it's different; it's in a way that it's okay. Because she does get to see you every day and she gets to know you in a way that she never did before. Do you understand this?
Brian and Treva: [Very emotional, they nod in agreement]
Krista: Are you getting headaches?
Brian: Yeah! I get a lot of headaches.
Krista: Do you recognize that a lot of this is from keeping things inside?
Brian: Mmm-Hmm.
Krista: It's like there's stress in your body and it feels like "contents under pressure." Do you understand that? [Brian nods in agreement] Know that she knows what you're going through.
Krista: Is there anything you want to ask her? Or anything you'd like to say to her?
[Misty bursts in to speak to Brian] *"Don't you dare say, 'I'm sorry!'"* As soon as I asked that, she pointed to you and said, *"Don't you dare say,' I'm sorry!"* [Tearful agreement from Brian]
Treva: Is she in a better place?
Krista: Oh yeah! Her Soul is forever! You will be able to connect with her from now until the end of time, because her Soul is forever.
Treva: When she left that day, did she know what was going to happen?
Krista: Maybe on the inside. She was hesitant about something that day. Because it's like, outwardly, no . . . It's like you know, but you don't know.
Brian: We just got a dog and this one right here [Pointing to the dog who greeted me at the door] did something funny at the time.
Krista: Is this the one that barks at nothing?
Brian: Yeah, that's the one, right here.
Krista: Okay. Know that when the dog looks in an area and barks, it's her.
Treva: I've had that happen. I've seen it.

Krista: Yeah, it's her. And you can talk to her. Everything is energy, and the reason that I stand up and move around when I'm reading is because it helps me pull my energy up, so that I can keep up with hers. It's very easy for them to mess with things like lights, television, and electricity. So, as time goes on and you practice connecting with her, you can ask her for things like that. Is this the area that the dog barks at? [Pointing to a corner of the room] Because I feel like I'm looking into a corner. Pay attention to where the dog looks when he does that, because that is her. Does that answer your question about the dog, that when the dog barks at nothing, it's her?

Brian: I just want her to be able to show herself; maybe not physically, but move things around or turn on some things.

Krista: And she can. Realize that as more time goes on, she becomes stronger. She's already a very strong energy, because I started getting things for you on the way here, but as soon as I walked in, she kept interrupting and she was ready! She already is very strong, just like in life, but know that you do keep your personality when you cross, which is good because then people know who they're connecting with. But as she goes through and learns more, she will learn how to do stuff like that. And I feel like I have to tell you to watch that light [Pointing to a light in the corner where I had felt her with the dog]. Also, it will get easier as you learn to connect more as well. My nephew died in 2007 and to this day my sister still cannot connect with him. But she is always in her head (always in drama); she is never just relaxing and feeling things. But I connect with him all the time. So, know that if you sit here and focus on connecting and getting her to make a light turn on, it's not going to happen. But when you get into a space where you're communicating with her, like a lot of times your hair will stand up or the temperature will change. When you start to feel things like that, know that it is her presence and the more time you spend there (in that presence), the more she'll start doing things like messing with lights and televisions, and bizarre stuff like that.

Treva: I just have a question about the wreck. So she didn't feel it?

Krista: She didn't. She says, *"It didn't hurt, mom."* It's the same sense of leaving your body. Is there a monument at the location? I feel like the location where this happened is permanently changed. Why is that?

Treva: It's all decorated.
Krista: [Seeing the crash site, I begin to set the scene] Was there some kind of a fence around that area?
Treva: Mmm-Hmm.
Krista: Was this tree involved in her accident?
Treva: Mmm-Hmm.
Krista: Okay. And there's a fence around it, or in front of it, or somewhere in that vicinity. Because I'm seeing some kind of a fence.
Treva: On the other side (of the tree). Actually, there are two fences; one over here, and one on the other side.
Krista: Was this a two-lane road?
Treva: Mmm-Hmm. It was a hill she knew very well.
Krista: Okay. Would it be accurate to say that the car would not turn when it needed to turn?
Brian: Or over-turned . . . she over-corrected when she turned the vehicle.
Krista: Oh, okay. Because I got the sense of a turn, but the car is not cooperating.
Treva: That's it! When you go over this hill, if you're going fast, you automatically go into the left lane. It's like a slight left.
Krista: Okay. I want to say this delicately: Have you made an enemy out of the other person's parents?
Treva: They never called.
Krista: Okay, so *they* made the enemy.
Treva: Mmm-Hmm. They never even called me.
Brian: They created an enemy.
Krista: I don't feel that she's with someone (from the accident). Did the other person not die?
Treva and Brian: [Both nod] No.
Krista: You're not thinking of suing them, are you?
Treva: [Shrugs her shoulders]
Krista: I have to do this [Covering my mouth with my hands]. To me, this means not knowing what to say. I don't feel that by them not contacting you, it was meant to hurt. I feel like it's more like: What do you say? I feel like if you choose to go that route, that's your choice, but know that she showed me that. And why do I feel like her friend is really torn?

Treva: Which friend?
Krista: Whoever was driving the car.
Treva: That girl has gone from day to day like she has done nothing.
Krista: But didn't the police records show she was going too fast?
Treva: Mmm-Hmm.
Krista: Yeah. I feel like she's not allowed to contact you. I feel like her parents are so worried about being sued that she can't come and talk to you. Her parents are worried that she's going to say something that's going to admit wrong. Do you understand this?
Treva: Mmm-Hmm.
Krista: Did you take something from the scene that night? You took something of hers, of your daughter's . . . something that was left there. What was it you took? I want to say her shoes.
Brian: Mmm-Hmm. Her shoes.
Krista: Was she not in them? It's like they were on her feet, but she came out of them.
Treva: Mmm-Hmm.
Krista: Who was the police officer that you knew was really shaken up about this?
Treva: That was Maker. Yeah, it really tore him up!
Krista: She really loved the way that he handled things! He came to her service, didn't he?
Treva: Yeah he did. When I spoke to him, he said that this girl will be charged. When he saw Misty, he actually had to sit down because in all his years as a State Trooper, this was the second worst wreck he's ever seen.
Krista: Was she not charged though? Because I feel like it didn't work out that way.
Treva: No. She hasn't been charged yet.
Krista: You feel her, don't you? [Directed to Brian] You feel her sometimes in your room when you're getting ready to go to bed.
Brian: [Nods in tearful agreement]
Krista: [Directed to Treva] That's the way you do it. Let him help you. Because I asked her what else she wanted to say and she showed me Brian in his room, feeling her and knowing it's her. So, know that she is with you; know that she is never gone. You just can't see her, but you can feel her. Brian feels her.

Brian: Something led me to learn the Law of Attraction.

Krista: Yeah. The more you delve into that type of stuff, the more your own awareness of Spirit will come up because it's all centered in spirituality.

Treva: Her dad said to tell her that he loves her. [Crying]

Krista: She called him Daddy. *"I love you too, Daddy. And I'm right here – I'm right here! I haven't gone anywhere."* She used to make you laugh, didn't she?

Treva: [Very emotional] She made everybody laugh.

Krista: Because she says, *"Remember me when you laugh . . . I'm right here."* Can I ask you: Are you remarried? Or are you still with her dad?

Treva: I'm still with her dad.

Krista: This is interesting because . . . [Trying to figure this out] Oh! Uncle! Uncle lives here!

Treva: Yes.

Krista: Okay because I felt the male authority figure . . . okay. She wants him to know that she's pulling for him. What is he going through? Is he struggling with something?

Treva: He's struggling with kidney stones.

Krista: What is it you have thought about doing? It's like you've thought about doing something. I don't know if it's seat belt awareness or something like that, but I feel like there's something you're wanting to do. [This felt like trying to implement a law, or dealing with local government]

Treva: Yeah! I want to change that hill over there. The hill they went over, I want to change it.

Krista: And you haven't worked on that yet, but you want to.

Treva: Yeah. That hill needs to be changed.

Krista: Please work on that. I feel like you don't have any direction right now.

Treva: Right.

Krista: I feel like you need something to focus on that you know is going to be good for your daughter and for other people and their kids. But she showed me; it was almost like a public awareness type of thing. So please do that. It would give you something positive to focus on, okay?

Treva: Mmm-Hmm.

Krista: She has an amazing smile! It's like she just lights everything up! To answer your question: I don't know if you've asked this question just in your own mind,

or if you've actually talked about it out loud . . . "How are we going to get through the holidays?" Did you express it outwardly?
Treva: Mmm-Hmm. Yep.
Krista: Are you setting a place for her at the table for the holidays?
Brian: Mmm-Hmm. For her birthday, too.
Treva: Yeah and for her birthday we're going to make her a cake.
Krista: Yes! She shows me that you're going to have a place for her, and she will be here. She'd never miss a holiday with you. And she says, *"I love you guys so much!"*

In speaking with Treva, at the writing of this book, more than a year after this reading, she informed me that just two nights before our reading, she had asked her brother, Darrell, "How are we going to get through the holidays? Misty never missed a holiday." During this same conversation, Treva also told me that Misty's sister had taken a drawing of Misty's and had it made into a tattoo to honor her sister and her many amazing talents.

Out of the entire reading, the things that stood out to Treva the most were; Misty talking about watching her mom cook, as just two hours before the crash, Misty sat in the kitchen and gazed (almost in awe) at Treva cooking supper for her family; and the stuffed animal that Misty mentioned in the reading. She had it her whole life, and Treva placed it in her casket, so Misty would always have it with her.

In Chapter 20, I have included a letter from Misty's mother, along with a poem written by Misty shortly before her passing.

You just can't make this stuff up!

Set A Place For Me At Thanksgiving

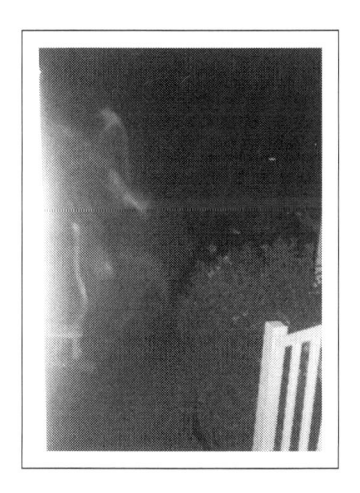

This is one of the most amazing Spirit photos I have ever seen! I wanted to really showcase this photograph, so please see the back cover for the full-color version and explanation of this photo.

Chapter 11
Someone has to talk about Charles

This photo was taken one week before Zachary's passing;
It was the last one ever taken of him.

Standing between the Worlds

In order to share this reading, I need to set the stage for you, and we will be going back one month prior to this reading. It was December 9, 2011. I was preparing for a gallery message service at a Mid-Tennessee bookstore, and, like always, I starting receiving messages while I was in the shower. I had a young man with me who kept calling out the name "Charles." At the time, I wasn't sure if this was his name or if he wanted to speak to or about someone named Charles.

I arrived at the bookstore and almost immediately began asking, "Who can take a Charles?" I asked this question a few times before I was told (by the young man in Spirit) "she's not here tonight," and then he was gone.

One month later, on Friday, January 10, 2012, I was back for another gallery message service at the same location. Somewhere about midway through this event, I felt that someone had lost a child, though I could tell the child was not young. I called out to the group of about fifty-five people, "Who lost a child? Someone lost a child." Immediately, I turned to face a woman sitting behind me; her name is Kimberly Nelms. I approached her and asked again, "Did you lose a child?" She swallowed hard, grasped the hand of her friend seated next to her, and nodded her head, "Yes." I responded, "You still have a girl" and Kim's eyes filled with tears as she spoke, "Yes, and I lost my son, Zachary."

In the instant that she spoke, I heard the name Charles once again. I recognized the energy as being the young man who came to visit me the prior month. I asked Kim, "Who is Charles?" She smiled and answered, "My husband." I told her about what had happened the month before and asked if she was supposed to come, but changed her mind at the last minute. She confirmed this with "Yes," as she laughed. Many people in the group who were there in December chimed in to say, "Yeah. She was asking about a Charles last month!" I asked Kim why she had not attended in December and she laughed and said, "Because Charles wouldn't let me."

I told her that Zachary wanted to talk to her about Charles. The message he relayed through me was that she was not "stuck" and that he supported her in whatever decision she wanted to make . . . but that "life is too short to be unhappy." Kim nodded in quiet agreement, knowing for certain that this message was coming from her son.

In an instant, he showed himself to me; he showed me that he had taken his own life. Zachary talked about his struggles with the opposite sex and how he was "so stupid" for doing what he had done. He comforted his mother and walked her through some memories, first of his death (which I will not reveal in this book), and then, of his life. He showed me his favorite autographed football by the Vanderbilt Commodores, his bedroom growing up, his relationship with his sister, and many of the things he liked to do.

Most importantly, Zachary apologized to his mom and assured her that she could not have done anything to prevent it. He did not want her to have any guilt about his decision to end his life. (Kim later revealed that this was a huge concern for her and that she had always wondered if she could have done something to prevent it). He was genuinely sorry to have hurt her so much. Before ending this message, Zachary told his mom how very much he loves her and he assured her that he is always here with her.

This was such a beautiful and touching moment for everyone in attendance that night. This message lasted about ten or fifteen minutes, as Zachary shifted back and forth from his cute and funny side, to his soft, loving, compassionate side. We all watched as Kim laughed, as she cried, and as she laughed and cried at the same time. You could feel their love for one another; this love filled the entire room and I knew that a deep healing was taking place within her. I don't believe there was a dry eye in the place as Zachary reached right into the heart of his mother and began to put her back together again!

You just can't make this stuff up!

A few weeks after connecting with Zachary at the gallery message service, I received the following Facebook message from Kim:

Hi Krista, I look forward to hearing the song you have for me. You really helped me the other night, and I thank you for that dearly. I found the courage to face some things that I had not been able to deal with since my son's passing (a year and a half ago). I read his death certificate for the first time on Sunday (two days after our connection). I found the strength to hold my son's ashes for the first time, and I will tell you it felt good to have him in my arms. All the memories play through my head like an old movie, which held all the precious moments that we shared together. I know I will always miss my son, but I also know that it was his time, and that it was his choice. I miss him so much each and every day, it's like part of my heart is empty now!

Zachary wanted to spend the time with me that I had wanted for so long. He was becoming a man. I was so proud of the things he was accomplishing; he had just moved into his new apartment just months before and he was so excited to be able to do it on his own. We celebrated his daughter, Cadence's Birthday the Saturday before; we had such a good time swimming and spending time together. I even took him to the grocery store that night before Cadence and I left his apartment to come home. I called him back on Sunday morning and told him I was coming to get him and we were going to be grilling out that day. I wanted him and Cadence to have time together that day.

Zachary would usually get frustrated because Cadence didn't want to leave my side for very long.

On this Sunday in June, it was like he was disconnected from us, so I asked him, "Zachary did you not want to come over here today?" He said, "Yes mom. There is just a lot of drama" (with Cadence's mom). When I took him home that Sunday night, he wanted us to stay longer and I really wish I had now, but I told Cadence's mom that I would have her back at a certain time. So I told Zachary that I couldn't; he stated he knew, but that it hurt. Before we left, I told my son that I loved him and that I would talk to him later. I hugged his neck and kissed his cheek.

Zachary was due to go to court for a child support hearing on Wednesday morning. I was supposed to pick him up and take him that morning, but I had forgotten. I drove to work in Nashville and only after a phone call from Cadence's mom, wanting to know where Zack was and telling me that he wasn't in the court room, did I realize that I had forgotten something.

I started calling and leaving messages. Zachary would always call me back eventually . . . but he wasn't. I called his work and found out he hadn't been there for a couple of days. A couple of hours passed and I still hadn't spoken with him, so I called the apartment manager, whom we had been swimming with the

Saturday before, to see if she had seen him. She said she would check and have the handyman go and knock on his door; but still no Zachary.

At this point, I decided to go to his apartment and told my daughter that I was going, so she came to my work and rode with me. I knew I had a key to Zachary's apartment at home and if I needed it, I could go home and get it.

When we got to his apartment complex, I stopped and told the property manager, Santee that I was going to Zack's apartment. She said she was going with me. When I got to his apartment, I knocked on his door as I called his name, but he didn't answer. I knew that my thoughts were correct and something was wrong . . . it was very wrong! I asked Santee if she had a key to his apartment that I could use to get inside. But she told me that she couldn't give me a key or let me in. Santee wanted to know why I thought something was wrong. All I could tell her was, **"I just know something's wrong!"** After hearing the sound in my voice and seeing the look on my face, Santee went to the office and got the key for Zachary's apartment. On her return, she told me again that I couldn't go in and not to follow behind her, to wait right where I stood, which was frozen right in front of the door. I nodded, and watched as she opened the door and started up the stairs, calling his name to let him know that she was inside. She was expecting Zack to jump out at any moment with a towel wrapped around him from the shower, since he was such a prankster . . . but not today! As Santee got further up the stairs leading to the living/dining area of the apartment, my heart sank further. Santee was almost at the top of the stairs when she gasped and ran back to the bottom! At this point, I knew my worst fear was true; my son had hung himself!

I knew Santee was my angel that day, and that it wasn't meant for me to see him hanging from the ceiling fan in the apartment! Krista, I felt the need to share my story with you today, and if you have gotten this far; I thank you for listening.

Kim

Standing between the Worlds

Sometimes Kim catches orbs in photographs, other times, it's streaks of light, like this one.

Chapter 12
I've got the Dog!

Krista: I'VE WRITTEN DOWN SOME THINGS FOR you, and the order seems to be important. Can I ask who is with you in Spirit that would relate to Jesus?
Dustin: Probably my grandpa and my mom.
Krista: Okay. I think it's the mom because when you said "mom," every hair on my body stood up. And can I ask you: I was writing something down, and I got a month and I didn't know if it was the month of March or the month of May. I got a month with an M. And when I wrote it, I was in my garage, and there was a dog leash that fell right off the wall . . . but it has been hanging on the wall for over a month, and it just fell for no reason. So, which one of those people would relate to March or May and have a tight affiliation with dogs?
Dustin: No, because when my mom passed, I was eleven. It was me, my mom, my brother and our stepdad. And my mom was born in July, and she actually passed in July. But the thing is we used to have a dog. His name was Beau, and he was actually killed in March of the year before – like a few months before my mom died.
Krista: [This is where March comes in] Okay. As you talk about your mom, are your hairs standing up?
Dustin: Yeah, a little bit.
Krista: You have never connected with her before, have you?
Dustin: No.
Krista: Can I tell you that she is with the dog?
Dustin: [Laughing] That doesn't surprise me at all.

Krista: She loves this dog! It was just so bizarre because that leash has hung there forever. I don't even use it for my dog anymore. And she relates well to Jesus, correct?

Dustin: Yeah, I believe so.

Krista: Oh, my word! She just wants to talk here: *"I have missed you so much! I have missed you so much!"* Are you the little brother?

Dustin: [Emotional moment] Yeah. My elder brother is thirty-one.

Krista: You have never gotten over that. I am sorry. She says that you don't remember things. Are you forgetting her, or forgetting details about her?

Dustin: Yeah, and there is a lot of confusion. I mean, I remember some stuff, but I was actually talking to my brother just the other day, saying that I don't remember a lot of details of her, just because I was so little.

Krista: Well, know that for her to tell me that, she is watching you. She is with you all the time. And can I ask you why my attention is drawn to her head?

Dustin: That I would not be sure.

Krista: I can't stop touching my head and I don't know if she lost her hair, if she loved her hair, she hated her hair, or if she hit her head. I don't know what it is; I can't place it, so I am just going to ask her for that. We will come back to it. What is her name please?

Dustin: Laura.

Krista: I have to tell you, even though there is no physical in Spirit, what she says is, *"This really does my heart good to come and talk to you today."* Would you understand that?

Dustin: [Crying] Yeah.

Krista: And she said that you wanted this. I don't know if you've been wanting or thinking about doing something like this (consulting with a medium) for a while, but you have been very unsure. Do you understand that?

Dustin: Yeah. I occasionally thought about it before, and then I just kind of made the decision just the other day. I was looking into it, and then thought "What the heck? Why not?" I thought about it every once in a while for years though.

Krista: Can I ask you: Was this dog the size of a German Shepherd? Or did it just have a lot of hair like a German Shepherd? Because she keeps showing me this damn dog, and he feels like a Shepherd!

Dustin: Yeah, it would have been. He was half black lab, half Australian shepherd. Yeah, he was all black and he was a pretty big dog.

Krista: So now that we've gotten that out of the way, I have to start at the top of the page now, because she just had to come through and let you know she's with the dog. And know that the things that I am saying to you are coming from her. Who wore suspenders? I don't know if this is someone in Spirit or someone in life, but I am being shown suspenders. Sometimes that's a sign for me of a farmer, and sometimes it's literally suspenders. But I just got suspenders, and that came from her.

Dustin: Her dad. He was on a farm.

Krista: Is he the one in Spirit with her?

Dustin: No. That's my dad's dad.

Krista: Okay, so when I asked if he is in Spirit with her, I got her blowing kisses. Is there a birthday or anniversary coming up for him? Because she is sending kisses to him.

Dustin: My grandpa?

Krista: Yeah.

Dustin: I think my grandpa's birthday is coming up, and I think their anniversary may be coming up in October.

Krista: Okay, because she is just blowing the kisses. So please tell him Happy Birthday. Now we're going to start my list, okay?

Dustin: Okay.

Krista: The first thing that I wrote down for you was: "new job." And then I had to cross it out and write "career," and "undecided path." Are you trying to figure out what you're going to do with your life, career wise?

Dustin: Yeah. Right now I'm in a limbo stage, and I hate it! I absolutely hate it. I hate not knowing.

Krista: Are you looking – and it doesn't have to be *exact*, it could be like the idea of – but what I wrote was: "work four days on, three days off." That could either be indicative of like a particular type of job, or it could be that you just want to make sure you have plenty of time off, but with full-time pay.

Dustin: Well, the job I do have now actually is only part time, but I typically work like three or four days a week.

Krista: Oh, okay, so that's what that is. The next thing is that you're trying to make up your mind; you're deciding. And it's about something personal. Personal either means a relationship or work. So what is it you are trying to make up your mind about? Relationship as well as work, right?
Dustin: Yeah, both.
Krista: Okay. What is the "cold feet" about? Because my feet are cold. And it happened out of nowhere, my feet just started freezing.
Dustin: [Laughing] Yeah, about five minutes before I called in, it must have gotten really cold and I needed to put on socks.
Krista: [Laughing] Okay. So just know that this is your mother's way of letting you know that even before you made this call, she was making sure that the two of us connected, and that's her way of telling me what's happening with you. She says that you're very serious, yet laid-back, and you are looking for a job where your work is your play.
Dustin: Yeah, kind of.
Krista: Because to you, if you have a job you love, then you don't really need to play, right?
Dustin: Right.
Krista: I know you are going to have questions for your mother, but I am supposed to ask you about your relationship with your father. Did you have issues with your father?
Dustin: I still do have issues with my father.
Krista: Okay. Listen to what was written right underneath that: "Who is the extremist or the person you think is very extreme?" Is that your father?
Dustin: Yeah.
Krista: Okay, because it's almost like there is no middle ground, where you like that middle ground, don't you? You are serious, yet also laidback?
Dustin: Yeah.
Krista: And I feel like his behavior or his moods are very extreme, or at least they appear that way. Do you understand this?
Dustin: Yeah. I've always described him as a very moody person.
Krista: Okay. Can I ask you: Do you analyze or observe? You like to sum people up.
Dustin: Kind of, I guess.

I've Got The Dog!

Krista: It could just be about the way that you analyze things. And can I ask you: This relationship that you're wondering about; is this the really free-Spirited person?
Dustin: Yeah, more Spirited than anyone I have been with before.
Krista: You know on a deep level that this is actually really good for you, don't you?
Dustin: Yeah, I think so.
Krista: What's her name, please?
Dustin: The girl that I'm seeing is Amber.
Krista: I get that she has something you want, like that free-Spirited thing. And you have something she needs, which is that grounded part that can really achieve things, like more disciplined.
Dustin: Mmm-hmm.
Krista: Together, you are a nice match, even if sometimes you piss each other off. It's about balance with the two of you. Because I get that you don't . . . and I don't know which one of you, but one of you doesn't really always know how you feel. Is that you or her?
Dustin: Probably both of us. More so her right now, because she kind of had an ex-boyfriend come into picture who she really cares about. But she tells me that she is really confused about her feelings for both of us.
Krista: Did your dad smother your mother? (Not meant literally) Because I was about to say something and your mother said, *"Don't smother her!"* Did your dad do that to your mother? Or maybe it was your stepfather that smothered her, because I feel like she knows what that's like. This may be something your brother can confirm for you (since he was so young). But I was about to tell you how to approach things with Amber, and she came right in saying, *"Don't smother her!"* So know, Dustin, that when you chase something, it runs.
Dustin: Right.
Krista: But at the same time, you don't want to give the impression that you don't care either. So it's about finding that comfortable place where you're like, "Hey, I am here . . . but I am not going to be your doormat." And can I ask: Did she not have a lot of stability in her life? [Talking about Amber]
Dustin: No, not at all. She actually got married and didn't end up finishing high school because she got pregnant. And then her dad passed away four years ago.

And then she ended up having some more kids with that same guy, and now they're not together anymore. And then, her mom passed away about a month ago. So she really doesn't have a lot of stability. But my mom and her mom are really, really good friends, and that's how I know her.
Krista: When you said that her mom passed away, once again, every hair on my body went up, and I was going to ask you: Is she a lot like your mom?
Dustin: Yeah.
Krista: I don't know if this is breast cancer. Was it her mom who had female cancer?
Dustin: Yeah. She had ovarian cancer.
Krista: Ovarian cancer, okay, so it's female cancer. So, she (Amber) is in a big way kind of lost. Did her mother teach her how to be a mommy?
Dustin: I think so, yeah.
Krista: Know that her mother is very proud of her, and she says that she did this against all odds. And why do I feel like she escaped the relationship with her ex?
Dustin: I know he was really not good.
Krista: He was emotionally abusive.
Dustin: Yeah.
Krista: So that would be the escape, okay. Your mom shows me Spirit with you as a child. So, that would be indicative of your mom passing when you were a child. And did you use to think that you felt her or dreamed of her? [Asking about when he was a child]
Dustin: I don't know, but I have always had the theory that I know she is there. I have always known she is watching over me. And I have kind of felt like maybe she sacrificed herself. Like when I was a really little kid and I would get sick or something; all she ever wanted to do was just take that sickness away from me, like she would want it on herself, so that I could be okay. And when we lived in another state and the people that I was hanging out with, they went on to be not very good people. And after her accident, I had to move in with my dad. That got me out of there and I had a great upbringing. I have never been in trouble with the law, and I have never done any drug. I don't really drink alcohol. And so I just feel like she made a deal with God that she wanted to better my life, so I don't know if she saw that it was not heading to a good place and she sacrificed herself to better my life.

Krista: Don't be surprised by things like that, because I've seen amazing things that happen in just that way. She always wanted the best for you, and she worked her butt off. I don't know if that means she had two jobs or if it was the kind of job she had, but she busted her butt.
Dustin: Yeah, because they worked in road construction.
Krista: Oh, okay. That's definitely busting her butt! Was she hit? Like an impact type of thing?
Dustin: Yeah, they were in a car accident. It was a single-car accident.
Krista: Okay, so now I am back to touching my head. Did she have a head injury in the accident? Because as soon as you said that, my hand is back to my head.
Dustin: Yeah. I mean they headed to Monte Carlo. That's when it happened; and it rolled a lot. And there were three people in the car, and all of them were thrown from the car, and all of them were killed. I am not sure exactly what happened. I am sure she probably had some sort of head trauma from it, but I am not aware of it all.
Krista: Yes, this is head trauma, and it's the same spot on the head I have to keep touching. Can I ask you how you relate to nature?
Dustin: What like animals? Or being outside?
Krista: Well, that's what I wrote: "How do you relate to nature?" And I feel like you don't have enough nature in your life. I don't know if that means animals, if that means mountains or water, or just being outdoors. But I feel like nature is the place where you feel really peaceful and like everything is good.
Dustin: Yeah, I hunt and stuff, but it's only once a year. I live in the middle of fifteen acres of trees.
Krista: Oh, okay. You do not spend enough time actually outdoors, though. Because it feels like you need more nature; you need more time with nature.
Dustin: Well, even living on these fifteen acres of trees, I haven't really been able to go out and explore too much. I have only been out once, so that's what I'm missing. I love walking around in trees and doing stuff like that, but I haven't done it.
Krista: Okay. Have you recently moved?
Dustin: I moved down here from Illinois in March or in May.
Krista: Oh wow! There's that March or May again. [Laughing] Do you know how much your mom wanted you to find me?

Dustin: I don't know, I guess. My cousin watches shows about this all the time, and it got me thinking about it, and then I looked it up and found you, and decided to call.

Krista: Do you understand that you were her baby boy? Did she always call you her baby? Or was it just that she babied you? Because she says, *"He is still my baby boy."*

Dustin: I'm not sure.

Krista: You may have to ask your brother because I feel like your brother would say, "Yes, she spoiled him rotten!"

Dustin: Oh yeah! [Laughing]

Krista: I don't know if you know this, because you were younger; but do you remember her tucking you into bed? Because she is showing this to me. She's showing she's tucking you into bed.

Dustin: [Tearful moment] Yes, I do.

Krista: Please don't ever forget that. And it's like, no matter what the day brought, no matter how busy or stressful, that was the time, where for those brief moments, everything was good. Do you understand that?

Dustin: [Crying] Yes, and she always said that too.

Krista: Yes. And it was like she would say, "tuck-tuck-tuck-tuck-tuck" when she tucked you in.

Dustin: [Laughing and crying] Yeah. And it was like blankets fully tucked underneath me.

Krista: Yeah, like a taco, all wrapped up. Did you sleep with socks on your feet or you are sleeping with socks now, because I'm seeing socks?

Dustin: I don't sleep with socks on my feet, very, very rarely. I hate it!

Krista: Did you do it then when you were little? Because I just keep seeing the socks.

Dustin: That I am not sure of.

Krista: Okay. Do you have any questions for your mom or your grandpa? And I have to tell you, he is very patient. He is just sitting here waiting.

Dustin: Grandpa?

Krista: Yeah, because this is your mom's time and he knows that.

Dustin: Yeah.

Krista: And he says, *"This is the best gift you could have ever gotten."*

I've Got The Dog!

Dustin: That's what my grandpa said?

Krista: Yes, and it's like this is *your* time. As soon as he says, *"This is the best gift you could have ever gotten,"* I see an actual present . . . and socks again! Was there a specific gift that he gave you that you still have or that you really, really loved because he is showing me a gift?

Dustin: I don't know if this would have anything to do with it, but I remember he always used to get me socks for Christmas.

Krista: Oh, my gosh! You are kidding! And see, he came right after the socks. [Laughing]

Dustin: Yeah. [Laughing]

Krista: Well, he is very patient and just letting your mother talk. Do you have any question?

Dustin: Let's see. I don't know

Krista: As soon as you said that – again, every hair stood up, and she says, *"I just love you so much."* It's almost like that's all that matters. And are you looking at getting a puppy?

Dustin: No, not really.

Krista: Well, I'm going to tell you that there is going to be a dog that's going to come into your plane, and it's going to be just exactly what you need. It's this year, but I don't know when. But I feel like you are going to get a dog very soon, and it's going to be exactly what you need. As far as your work, why are your hands important to your work?

Dustin: I run a camera.

Krista: You are really creative, but you are looking for something different, and I don't understand what that is. I don't know if it's a totally different line of work, or going to the next level, but she just showed me that your hands are very important to your work.

Dustin: Well, I am going to be a volunteer assistant basketball coach, men's basketball. So that's an unpaid thing, and financially, I'm going to be giving up a lot to do that. And if that works out, then hopefully I will go back to school and get my master's, while still coaching. Then I will have three years of assistant coaching, and hopefully after that, I can actually find a paid position as an assistant basketball coach. But I feel like I'm stuck between that and just trying to do this film stuff. The film stuff down here is hit or miss; it's a lot of freelance and it's just hard to get it started. So, I'm still stuck between: Do I go with the basketball thing, or do I go with film?

Krista: She says to keep your passion your passion. You are actually very fortunate because people can either be very business-minded or very creative, and you're kind of both. She says, *"Why not keep your passion your passion?"* And that's really interesting because I am a Life Coach as well, and one of the things that I always end up telling people is to follow your passion and it will take care of you financially. So I think this is the first time ever that I have told someone – well, your mom did, actually – to *not* make their passion their work, but your mother is saying to keep your passion your passion. And this is about taking care of *yourself* and making sure that you're supported financially. Now I'm interested in the emphasis on that word 'yourself.' She wasn't able to provide for herself, was she?

Dustin: No, not really.

Krista: Because this feels like "don't do what I did!" She was very creative as well, wasn't she?

Dustin: Yeah.

Krista: And she could never be fit into a box. She was like this ultimate nonconformist, which is very good, but she said that's where she struggled the most. So she had this passion that she didn't get to live because she didn't make plans to take care of herself, and she wants to make sure that you are taken care of, without having to rely on anyone else.

Dustin: Okay.

Krista: She wants to hug you. Just know that she's just hugging you right now; she gave you bear hugs, big hugs. I don't know if it's the way she hugged you or the way you hugged her, but it's like this is the "she doesn't want to let go" type of hug. And it's indicative of the way that you hugged when she was here.

Dustin: [Tearful] Oh, yeah!

Dustin called me a few hours after our reading to tell me that his girlfriend called him from the animal rescue, where she was picking out a new dog for the two of them.

You just can't make this stuff up!

Chapter 13
Are You having Twins?

Krista: It's interesting the way that this works because when I know that I am going to do a reading, I start getting things before I see you. And I have to tell you that right before you came, I started having problems with my vision. Are you having problems with your vision?
Presley: Oh, yeah! I am legally blind!
Krista: Okay. Has your left eye been giving you problems or are you due for a check up on that?
Presley: Yeah, my left eye is getting worse.
Krista: Okay. So after I got off phone with you when you scheduled your reading, I looked at my friend and said, "Oh my goodness, I have a new baby for Presley!" Are you looking to have another child?
Presley: Yes! [Laughing]
Krista: I have another child coming for you, yes.
Presley: So we *are* going to have it?
Krista: You are, and it's going to come within two years.
Presley: That's exactly what my aunt said. She's the only one I have ever told because I am scared to death to tell anybody else.
Krista: I do have a child for you. And you already have one male, correct?
Presley: Yeah.
Krista: This is interesting because when I first started reading professionally, I always got my baby energy wrong. Any time I said female, it was always male; and any time I said male, it was a female. Then, all of the sudden, I got it right. But for you, I get female *and then* I get male. Are you wanting twins? Or would you like twins?

Standing between the Worlds

Presley: [Laughing] I was going to do the IVF and it is more likely for twins, yes.
Krista: Okay, because it's like it keeps changing; girl, boy, girl, boy, girl, boy. So I do have that for you and it's going to be within two years. I'm not sure if this is twins, or if you get pregnant, but the first time, it doesn't keep. Do you understand? And do you have a graduation or something coming up soon?
Presley: I do . . . yeah.
Krista: Okay. And this is a career path, correct?
Presley: Yes.
Krista: This is medical.
Presley: Yeah.
Krista: Okay. Do you understand that when you get done, that you will go one place and then have to go another; like you won't jump into your dream place the first time?
Presley: Yeah.
Krista: But I have to give you that right at that same time, when the whole rest of your life is changing, is when you're going to have that dream place. And I feel like you're going to be backing up. Let me see what this is about . . . [Pausing to speak with Spirit] So it must be like a leave of absence when you have the baby or babies, or possibly you will change your mind on career altogether. But know that you are not going to struggle. And are you wanting to work with children if you stay in the medical field?
Presley: I wanted to work with babies. When I graduate from nursing school, I thought about going into . . .
Krista: [Interrupts] NICU.
Presley: Yeah. [Laughing]
Krista: I really have to give that to you that you are going to need to get your feet wet first. It's something a little different, a little broader, and that's going to help you to discern really what you want, because I feel like you're unsure. [Back to the baby] And would you understand that there is a large potential that you would have a cesarean?
Presley: No, although I had a hard time with a six pound baby. I practically bled to death, so I can imagine.

Are You Having Twins?

Krista: I have to give you cesarean and I don't feel like it's scheduled. I feel like it's going to be something like you are going to try to go natural and then it's going to be like . . . not happening! But don't worry, nothing's wrong with the baby . . . babies. I really just feel like it's babies – plural. So, when it happens, don't freak out. You will anyway, because you will totally forget that I said this, but someone would go, "Now remember, she told you they are going to be fine. Don't freak out!"

Presley: Yeah. [Laughing]

Krista: Are you planning on being present there? [Directed to her friend, Karla, who was in the room during the reading] Are you like a coach or something like that with her?

Karla: Always.

Krista: Because I feel like you are going to be part of her whole thing. And what's coming in June or July?

Presley: My daughter's birthdays. I have two daughters and it's both of their birthdays.

Krista: So is it June or July?

Presley: June.

Krista: Okay but is it towards July, like the end of June. And is someone a princess? One of your daughters?

Presley: A princess? Yes. [Laughing]

Krista: Is one a princess and one is more of a tomboy?

Presley: Yeah, exactly! [Laughing]

Krista: And the tomboy is easier.

Presley: Yeah.

Krista: And the other one's kind of like a drama queen?

Presley: Oh yeah! [Laughing]

Krista: And I am feeling like she would scream bloody murder, cry at the top of her lungs because someone hit her; but as soon as that person gets in trouble, she stops crying.

Presley: Yeah! [Laughing]

Krista: There is a woman around this child. Is this the younger girl or the older girl?

Presley: The older one is the drama queen. The younger one is the easy one; she is nine years child.
Krista: Because with the older one, there is someone around her that I don't feel was here when the other one was born; or that the other one wouldn't remember. I don't know what that means.
Presley: I do. My grandma . . . who died.
Krista: She died after one was born, and before the other.
Presley: Yeah.
Krista: Okay. Have you resolved your issues with your mother?
Presley: No, never! [Laughing]
Krista: And it's funny because she says, *"I am her mother."*
Presley: Exactly! I told her that. I called her "momma."
Krista: She is your mother, okay. Which one of your daughters is like your mother in temperament?
Presley: Hope, the oldest one.
Krista: And just today she reminded you of your mother, right?
Presley: Yeah. [Laughing]
Krista: Yeah, she's telling me this. Who has or had a cat?
Presley: I do. I had a cat that just died.
Krista: Is there a black cat?
Presley: I have a black cat; I just bought one.
Krista: Okay. And was that supposed to replace the other cat.
Presley: Yeah. And I am pretty attached to my cat.
Krista: Yes, you are. She's showing me the black cat and this is interesting because your grandmother really bought into the wives tales about black cats. You know that, right?
Presley: Yeah. [Laughing]
Krista: And so she is sitting here telling me about how you can't change litter when you're pregnant, and to be careful that the cat doesn't smell milk on the baby, and just all that kind of junk. [Laughing]
Presley: That's exactly how she was, like super superstitious! [Laughing]

Krista: Oh yeah, like all of this weird stuff and she is just warning you about it. You were there when she crossed.
Presley: Yeah, I was. [Tearful]
Krista: Did you touch her face like this? [I demonstrate stroking the cheek]
Presley: No, I was holding her. I was like lying across her.
Krista: And you touched her face, because I had to sit here and touch my face. Do you know that you were her world?
Presley: Yes, I did do that. And I know I was.
Krista: And she is really, really proud of you. And of course she has to take credit for it. [Laughing] She says, *"I did good."* She did good; because she raised you . . . she did *really* good! And she says that there was a time that it was questionable. [Laughing]
Presley: Oh yes! [Laughing]
Krista: There was a time that she didn't know if you were going to be the death of her. She worried and worried about you. What was your involvement with the motorcycle?
Presley: I had a motorcycle when I was fourteen and I rode it. Nobody knows that either. [Laughing] I still have a motorcycle.
Krista: Because when she was talking about you and how she thought you would be the death of her, she brings up you on a motorcycle. So she knew!
Presley: Yeah. Nobody would ever think that. [Laughing]
Krista: Did she have skin tears?
Presley: Yes.
Krista: And you put stuff on them, didn't you? You rubbed stuff on her skin.
Presley: Yeah. She used to have them on her legs and arms. Her skin would tear so easy. [Crying]
Krista: Yeah, and you took care of it; you nursed it. And that's why you want to be a nurse. Do you recognize that you have money coming up for you? Are you expecting money?
Presley: I hope so . . . from a lawsuit, yeah.
Krista: Yes, you are going to get it.

Presley: Well, it's for my son, not for me.
Krista: But you are going to get it. I have to tell you that it is going to come. And it feels like was it a "negligence" thing.
Presley: Yeah. [Surprised]
Krista: She says you are going to get it. And that they've been raking you through the coals. But you are going to do well with it. And were you planning on getting another car when you do?
Presley: Well it would be for my son, so probably not. I want another car, but I just bought a new car.
Krista: Okay, but I still see a new car. I can't let that go. And she tells me that you take care of your son. So really, it goes to you in the way that you see fit. But not to be a martyr and leave you out, because that's what she did.
Presley: Well, all of my money goes to them anyway. But yeah, she gave everything she had to me, and I do the same to my kids. Should I sell my house?
Krista: Are you between selling it and remodeling it?
Presley: Yes! [Surprised]
Krista: She says you've got the stability where you're at. And she says to put the money in what you already have.
Presley: I do have a lot of stability.
Krista: You do.
Presley: So, I should not move?
Krista: No. She doesn't see you moving. She quite likes your house. Do you have a wooden thing out back, like wooden steps or something?
Presley: We have steps in my house. I am sure they're wood.
Krista: No, like outside. Is there a deck with wooden steps going to the ground?
Presley: Oh yeah! [Laughing] I have massive wooden stairs to go to my deck, probably like yours.
Krista: Yes, that's what I was seeing. She loves that.
Presley: I connect with her when I am on my deck.
Krista: Well, no wonder she loves it. [Laughing] Yes, and she is there a lot; she loves that. And do you recognize the view of the sky is beautiful from there?
Presley: Yeah.
Krista: And she is there as well. Is there a star that you look at in particular that makes you think of her?

Presley: Yes! [Surprised] Because the right side is all trees, but the left side is all open. So it's all on that left side. You can't see anything on the right side.
Krista: And there is one star that's blue, and it gets your attention. And she says, *"I am shining down on you."* So, know that your draw to that star is about your connection with her. But that's her favorite place and she just wouldn't want you to sell it. You are not happy with your bathroom, are you?
Presley: No. I hate my bathroom.
Krista: Was one of the things you wanted a Jacuzzi or something?
Presley: Well I have one but I never get to use it.
Krista: Is your Jacuzzi on your deck? Where is your Jacuzzi?
Presley: In the bathroom.
Krista: Well, she talked about a Jacuzzi or something, but I felt like it was out back. So I thought maybe she was saying . . .
Presley: [Excitedly interrupts] Oh! We are thinking about putting a pool in the backyard if we stay.
Krista: Okay. [Laughing] If you do that, don't do the above ground. She says they are cheap.
Presley: Oh that's what we are going to do. Yeah she was like that. [Laughing]
Krista: She doesn't mind paying for quality.
Presley: Yeah.
Krista: But she valued what she valued, right? And she knows that you get what you pay for. And she says, *"That car was paid off. You may laugh, but it was paid for."* Were you in some kind of an accident or something and you hurt your shoulder or neck? Because I feel like my neck and shoulder are very stiff.
Presley: Yep. That's me.
Krista: And you didn't have that looked at, or you didn't take care of it properly.
Presley: Yeah, I'm supposed to have surgery, but I have been putting it off.
Krista: Here is what she says about the surgery: *"If you take your car to a mechanic, they'll tell you something is wrong."* It's almost like if you go to a doctor; they're going to find something wrong with you. And do you recognize she loves your husband?
Presley: Yeah.
Krista: She says, *"He is so good for you, and he does a lot."* And she didn't have the kind of freedom that you have. And she said, *"I could never go out and do this."* She could never just be gone, but you can, because you have got a great husband.

Presley: Yeah. [Laughing]
Krista: And did you have a quiz or test recently, where you didn't do as well as you thought?
Presley: Yeah.
Krista: Yes, but there was one that particularly upset you.
Presley: Yeah. [Laughing]
Krista: She wants you to let it go. She says that you're not going to have any problems getting through school. Were you wanting to go with your RN, and then maybe later come back and do more?
Presley: Yeah. I don't stop; I just keep going. I am like a professional student.
Krista: I understand. Is she the one who had arthritis in her hands?
Presley: I do.
Krista: You do, okay. And do you spend a lot of time on the computer?
Presley: Yeah.
Krista: Because I feel like my hands are so stiff . . . and you've got carpal tunnel, don't you?
Presley: Yeah. I have really bad swelling and stiffness.
Krista: But you don't take care of it.
Presley: No, I have arthritis everywhere. But my hands bother me the most.
Krista: They do, and it feels like it's going up my arm. Do you understand that it's related to your shoulder sometimes?
Presley: Yeah. It's all the way down at one side, the right side.
Krista: She was right handed.
Presley: Yeah.
Krista: Okay because it's like I am trying to hold something with my left hand, and I feel like I can't even do that right. It's really bizarre and it's her. She says you want to talk about your dad.
Presley: Yeah.
Krista: Okay. What would you like to know?
Presley: Does he love me?
Krista: She says, *"Of course he loves you, of course no one could love you like I love you."* You were her baby. She wants you to know that – in her own way – your mother does love you too. Is your mother not quite right?
Presley: No. No, she is not quite right. [Laughing]

Krista: Do you understand that your mother was troubled forever even before you . . . like her whole life?
Presley: Yeah.
Krista: Does she drink? Or what does she do that really screws up her life because it feels like it's compulsive?
Presley: Gambling, lying.
Krista: Does she go from boyfriend to boyfriend, or man to man?
Presley: [Laughing] I'll say! She's been married thirteen times!
Krista: *"And she ain't figured it out yet."* That's from grandma.
Presley: Nope! [Laughing]
Krista: That's what she says, *"She ain't figured out yet, and she probably never will."* And in her way, in the way that she is capable of – which is probably however your cat's capable of swimming – but in her way, she does love you . . . and so does your dad. She just doesn't love her, alright. Who was it who really messed up your dad emotionally?
Presley: Her.
Krista: Her, okay. Has he not been the same since then?
Presley: Right. It's almost like he hates me because of her.
Krista: He doesn't. Would you recognize that you've done better in your life than he has in his?
Presley: Yes.
Krista: And would you recognize that he actually is jealous of what you're capable of?
Presley: Yeah.
Krista: Really, honestly. And he could not provide.
Presley: I don't think he expected me to do as well as I have. I think it's that expectation (of failure) is how I feel.
Krista: Yes, absolutely. He expected you to be squashed and you weren't, and you just said, "Watch! I will show you! I will get ninety-seven different degrees." [Speaking of school]
Presley: Yeah. [Laughing]
Krista: So I feel like he's floundering. He just doesn't know how to focus. Does he start things and not finish them?
Presley: He never finishes anything!
Krista: Grandma says, *"You're perfect just the way you are."*

In summary, Presley and her husband received a windfall of unexpected money and bought a new BMW. Their lawsuit is still ongoing. Presley had in-vitro fertilization a few times over the next year and had a positive pregnancy test a year and a half later, on October 2, 2013. As of the writing of this book, it is still unknown if she's having twins.

You just can't make this stuff up!

Chapter 14
Don't give Your Power Away

Krista: Okay Deborah, I just wanted to sit down, but I couldn't because my body just wouldn't respond. And that that was you. What was the jolt you have had to your body? It feels like it was a long, long time ago.
Deborah: I had a slip and fall like ten years ago. So, yes, it has been a long time.
Krista: But do you recognize that the fall was the catalyst for all that goes on with you today?
Deborah: Oh yeah, definitely.
Krista: It's like you just weren't the same after that.
Deborah: Oh yeah.
Krista: Were you a waitress?
Deborah: Yeah. [Surprised]
Krista: And it really pretty much just ended that for you. It was like, "That's it! No more!" And did you hurt your wrist in the process as well?
Deborah: Yeah. I fell on my wrist, as I was trying to catch myself.
Krista: Does that ever bother you when it gets rainy?
Deborah: Yeah.
Krista: It's interesting. I keep clearing my throat. That means that there is something that needs to be said. Is there something that you need to say to someone and you are not saying it? Do you understand this, Deborah?
Deborah: Yeah. I think with a couple of people, yeah.
Krista: And I have to tell you that you were given your voice for a reason; use it. Don't be afraid to use it. Does that make sense to you?
Deborah: Yeah.

Krista: You have been through a lot of crap. I feel like you have really taken yourself from the gates of hell. Does this make sense to you?
Deborah: Yeah it does.
Krista: And was there an influence of people that were not good for you.
Deborah: Oh yes, of course.
Krista: And I almost feel like – and this could be whoever this is that you need to say something to – I almost feel like if I was going to speak for you, I would say something like, "You know what? I've been there; I'm not doing that again!" Do you understand this?
Deborah: Yeah!
Krista: So recognize that that's your power and not to give it away. I feel like you have given it away before. Do you have an uncle in Spirit?
Deborah: I do.
Krista: You weren't very close with him.
Deborah: Not really. He was my dad's brother.
Krista: Was there something in his abdomen? Or is there something with your abdomen?
Deborah: Yeah, mine.
Krista: Okay. And is it here? [Showing a place in my abdomen]
Deborah: Yeah. Actually yeah, both myself and my mother.
Krista: Okay. Was your uncle, disconnected geographically? Or just disconnected? Because he wants to talk about the disconnect. I don't know what that means.
Deborah: I don't know. I mean he lived basically right down the road. I am kind of thinking you might be talking about my other uncle, which is definitely a disconnect that I have nothing to do with, and he's alive though. It's my dad's other brother
Krista: I'm not sure, but the one that's here with you in Spirit, the one that you didn't really know very well; he wants to talk about this disconnect. Would you understand him wanting to talk about the other uncle?
Deborah: Yeah, I can understand that.
Krista: I know when I say this, that your first thought is going to be, "Hell no!" But I'm going to say it anyway and I don't want you to think about it like that. Do you have forgiveness work to do with this other uncle? Do you have something that you need to forgive him for?

Deborah: Yeah.

Krista: And the 'hell no' is that I understand why you don't want to forgive him. I get that and I know what this is about. That thing set you – I mean it was really, really huge! I know that he mistreated you. Do you understand that he didn't mistreat *just you*? Would it make sense to you that he is sick?

Deborah: Yeah. Yeah. [Tearful]

Krista: I stopped clearing my throat when we got to this subject and it occurred to me: Was there like a "shock?" Because I almost feel like . . . well, I feel like I'm shocked.

Deborah: A whole lot of shocks in my life.

Krista: Around the uncle.

Deborah: Yeah. I don't go near him. I don't want my kids around him. If I see him with my kid . . . at one time, yeah I did, and I think I went into a panic.

Krista: So there was a shock.

Deborah: Yeah. "Drop my kid now" is what I said.

Krista: This man [Indicating the uncle in Spirit] doesn't know me; you and I don't even know each other, but he knows what I've been through, because the Soul knows everything. I'm going to offer you a healing with all of this when we are done. And this will really, honestly separate your emotion from that memory, okay? Because I feel that you are at that time; you're ready.

Deborah: Yeah, okay. [Crying]

Krista: Do you have a mini-van?

Deborah: Yeah.

Krista: Do you need something done with your left, front tire? Do you need new tires?

Deborah: [Laughing] I just got new tires yesterday.

Krista: Okay. And was the left, front the one that was the worst?

Deborah: I think so, yeah. They were really pretty bad, but yeah.

Krista: You know you need an alignment as well?

Deborah: Yeah. I got it. It's all good now.

Krista: Okay good. Who went out with something in the chest? I feel like my chest is being crushed? And it's even a little difficult to breathe.

Deborah: My mom.

Krista: Was this lung cancer? Or cancer, but something with the lungs? What was this?

Deborah: She died of ovarian cancer, but it was all . . . [Crying] There was all the fluid in the lungs.
Krista: Sniff. Do you smell her? Do you smell your mother? I smell your mother.
Deborah: Yeah! [Excited]
Krista: This is still very raw for you. It was quick. It was really quick. Was she misdiagnosed or undiagnosed?
Deborah: Yeah I think so.
Krista: And then it wasn't until it was too late that she got the diagnosis. Did you take care of her?
Deborah: For that week, yeah. I mean we didn't realize how sick she was until after she went into the coma and the doctor said that it was ovarian cancer, not pneumonia. [Very emotional moment]
Krista: Do you feel like you didn't get to say goodbye?
Deborah: Yes.
Krista: So she wants you to know that you did. You talked to her, but you didn't know if she heard you and you held her hand. What did you do to her feet? Did you put socks on her feet?
Deborah: [Laughing and crying] Yeah, I put socks on her feet. I didn't want her feet to get cold.
Krista: So, recognize that she is showing me this. She knew that you were doing this. And did you pick out the flowers for her funeral? And did you choose the music? Because she says, *"They were lovely."* And that was her word 'lovely.' Has she not been gone very long? Or is it still just really fresh for you?
Deborah: Ten years ago, but yeah, it's still fresh.
Krista: What was five years ago? Did you have like a memorial or something five years ago? Did you go to her grave site? Because I'm getting five around this.
Deborah: Yeah, we go to the grave. It's been almost like what . . . [Thinking]
Krista: When did your dad remarry?
Deborah: Yeah, about five years ago. [Laughing]
Krista: And that's when he stopped going. Were you part of that wedding? Or who was?
Deborah: My daughter was.
Krista: Your daughter was part of the wedding, okay. Was it with the flowers?
Deborah: Yeah.

Krista: How or why did that wedding remind you of her funeral?
Deborah: It was at the same church.
Krista: What have you not said to your stepmother? Because here I go with my throat again.
Deborah: I really like my stepmother. I think that was just . . .
Krista: You didn't want him to get married that soon.
Deborah: Yeah, I had a problem with that. [Crying] I felt like it was dishonoring her memory.
Krista: [On my knees in front of her] Do you understand that he doesn't know how to be alone?
Deborah: Yeah, I can definitely understand that.
Krista: Do you understand that this is like filling a void?
Deborah: Yeah, I can see that.
Krista: I feel like he took it really hard when your mom passed away. It's like he didn't know how to live. What did he do; like he didn't want to live or he didn't . . . ?
Deborah: He got sick, actually.
Krista: Oh, okay. And there was a time in that where he just didn't care, "Just take me!" He just wanted to be with her. He had guilt with her. Do you understand that?
Deborah: Yeah I think I do. I think he didn't want to live. He blamed himself that he didn't get her to the doctor quicker; I think we both did; him and me both.
Krista: She says, *"There is nothing you could have done."* She is telling me the kind of cancer because there are so many different kinds. She is saying it was carcinoma; and it goes like phew . . . gone. [Indicating that it moved quickly] So, she says, *"There is nothing you could have done. It's just the way it was."* And was your mom busy-busy-busy? Because she says that her work here was done. She was done.
Deborah: Yeah.
Krista: You celebrated her birthday, didn't you?
Deborah: Yeah, I celebrated it this year.
Krista: And you make her favorite food.
Deborah: On her birthday, I try to make anything she made. It doesn't come out right though. [Laughing and crying]

Krista: I have something about Mother's Day with your husband; did he not really honor your mother on Mother's Day, and it bothered you? Mother's Day was significant for you after she crossed. What does that mean?

Deborah: I think he never really understood. Mother's Day is really hard on me and I don't think he really understood that because he wasn't close to his family and I was extremely close to my mom and dad. [Crying] He doesn't understand, like on February 25th, the day she died, that always hits me really hard. Mother's Day is difficult for me too.

Krista: Okay. And Christmas sucks.

Deborah: Yeah, because she loved Christmas! That was her favorite holiday, her favorite time.

Krista: And she went all out. She was the center of everything. And did the family kind of go their own ways when she died?

Deborah: Yeah.

Krista: You called her "Momma."

Deborah: Yeah.

Krista: You made her a promise, didn't you . . . when you were with her that week? Who did you promise to take care of? Because she is telling me that you made her a promise.

Deborah: She kept asking about her little dog, Greasley, and she made me promise that he would be fine. She wanted me to sneak him in the hospital . . . and before we knew it, she was dying. She loved that dog. [Crying]

Krista: Did you take her clothes? You still have some of them.

Deborah: Yeah.

Krista: And I feel like even the ones you didn't like, they still hang in your closet.

Deborah: Yeah. [Laughing and crying]

Krista: Do you know how to sew. Because I am getting that they wouldn't fit you.

Deborah: Yeah. She was really, really little so everything had to be altered.

Krista: And you know that dynamite comes in small packages. [Laughing]

Deborah: Yeah. [Laughing]

Krista: And that would be something that she would say because she was shorter than *everyone*.

Deborah: Yeah, pretty much. All her sisters are real short. I just never got the gene for some reason.

Krista: Did you do this with her? [Standing next to her, comparing height]

Deborah: [Laughing] Yeah, I always used to make fun of her.

Krista: Because she is showing me that. And you have a song for her. It's your song. Is that Celine Dion? I don't know why I have to give you this, but I have to give you the song, "Because You Loved Me." I have to give you that song.

Deborah: Yeah, I love that song!

Krista: Does that make you think of her?

Deborah: Yeah. There are so many songs that make me think of her, but that one too.

Krista: Are you having issues with your husband?

Deborah: Yes.

Krista: And do you feel like he always makes you wrong?

Deborah: Yeah, to a certain degree.

Krista: It's like, "No matter what the hell I do, it's never right, it's never enough!"

Deborah: Yeah.

Krista: You have two kids?

Deborah: Yeah.

Krista: Are you waiting for them to be gone before you leave?

Deborah: That might be, yeah. I mean that's been a mistake. I'm just kind of in limbo about it.

Krista: Do you have a boy and a girl?

Deborah: Two girls.

Krista: Is one a tomboy?

Deborah: Yeah, she is.

Krista: She dresses like a boy, long shorts and big T-shirts.

Deborah: Yeah. She loves basketball shorts and stuff like that.

Krista: Okay. And no, she is not gay. [Laughing] I know you are worried about that, but she is not. And is she almost a teenager?

Deborah: [Laughing] Yeah, I never told anyone that, but I was thinking about it just the other day! She is eleven, so yeah, almost a teenager.

Krista: Does your husband have a boat?

Krista: Yeah.

Krista: And do you hate that boat?

Deborah: With a passion! [Laughing]

Krista: Is that where his time and attention goes to?
Deborah: Yeah.
Krista: Why do you hate the boat?
Deborah: Because it's a big money-hole, he's always doing stuff with it, and it's ugly.
Krista: I feel like he doesn't use it.
Deborah: He doesn't. It just sits there.
Krista: Is he messy and you feel like you are cleaning up after him?
Deborah: Yes! [Laughing]
Krista: And you say, "Look at the yard! What are the neighbors going to think?"
Deborah: Yeah. [Laughing]
Krista: You have a lot of questions around finances. I know you have concerns about financial security. Is this just about if you are on your own? Or are things tight at this moment?
Deborah: I don't know and he never tells me.
Krista: So, *there* is your question around the finances. You really don't have a clue.
Deborah: No, I have no idea.
Krista: Do you know what a narcissist is?
Deborah: No. I have heard the word, but I don't really know what it means.
Krista: Narcissist is where everything that you do is a reflection on me. They act like they are very, very important . . . but the truth is they don't think they are important at all. It's like they come across as having a big ego, but really they just don't love themselves. Does that fit him? Because this is exactly what she is calling him, a narcissist.
Deborah: Yeah, he's a lot like that.
Krista: Did your mother read the Bible?
Deborah: Yes. She taught it in the school.
Krista: Because she is telling me – and this is about him, this is to him, not to you – she is saying, *"Pull the plank from your own eye before you acknowledge the thorn in mine."* Does that make sense for you with him?
Deborah: Yes! [Laughing]
Krista: Do you want to talk about the one that got away?
Deborah: Yeah. [Sighs]

Don't Give Your Power Away

Krista: I'm getting that there was someone that you were just absolutely head over heels, passionate, love with your heart and Soul. Did he drive you crazy?
Deborah: Yeah. [Laughing]
Krista: And did you ultimately end up making a decision to leave that behind?
Deborah: Yeah.
Krista: Do you still speak to him?
Deborah: Every now and then, yeah.
Krista: And it still makes your heart go pitter-patter! He is still available, isn't he?
Deborah: Yeah. [Laughing as if she's been "busted"]
Krista: Do you recognize that he is your Soul-mate?
Deborah: I never have really thought about it that way.
Krista: Did you think about that when you were with him?
Deborah: Yeah, I think maybe I did.
Krista: Do you recognize that there has been nobody before him or since him that elicited that kind of feeling in you?
Deborah: Oh yeah!
Krista: Definitely, definitely your Soul-mate! And I don't know if you want to hear this, but it's not over with the two of you. Does this make sense to you?
Deborah: I don't know . . . Oh boy!
Krista: At some point, there will be an opportunity for the two of you again. Does he apologize? Does he say, "I screwed up?"
Deborah: He has. I messed up, but I mean that was kind of it, you know; I messed up, and he apologized.
Krista: I have to give you that there is going to be an opportunity for that again, based on current path . . . but of course, we all have free will.
Deborah: Right.
Krista: You could make a totally different decision; you could get up and move to Moscow tomorrow. Not that you will, but you know what I mean. You and your husband could work your issues out and live happily ever after . . . but based on current path, that relationship could come up for you again. And, who reads books, you or your mother?
Deborah: My mom used to read.

Krista: Did she read to you when you were little? Did she have those Harlequin things? Did she read those romance novels or something?
Deborah: Yeah. She read a little bit of everything.
Krista: Did she trade books with people?
Deborah: Yeah, I think years and years ago.
Krista: Oh yeah. I am talking about when you were little.
Deborah: Yeah. I think her and her friends would read a book and then pass it off to each other.
Krista: And it's like Danielle Steel, and stuff like that.
Deborah: Yeah. [Surprised]
Krista: And I'm just going to tell you what I see, and I don't know if this was often, or if it was just once. I see that you are home and you are lying with her; she is on her side and you are on your side, and she's got her arms around you and she is reading her book because you fell asleep. Do you remember that?
Deborah: Yeah! [Laughing and very surprised]
Krista: She is showing me that she used to lay down with you to get you to take naps, but she still read her books. So she is showing me these things that you two shared in your life when she was here and also since she's passed. And do you still dream about her?
Deborah: Yeah.
Krista: Please know that they are not dreams . . . and you know that, don't you? They are not. And in your "dreams," does she suddenly come back and it's like, "Where have you been?"
Deborah: Yeah!
Krista: Those are not dreams and she is always, always with you. And do you have a brother? Who has a brother? She has a brother.
Deborah: Yeah, she has two brothers.
Krista: Still here.
Deborah: Yeah. Actually all of her siblings are still alive.
Krista: Which brother is this that she would visit?
Deborah: Mark.
Krista: Okay. Because she visits you and she visits with him.
Deborah: I can see that; Mark is really cool.

Krista: That was her favorite. I don't know if they were close in age, but she had a connection to him. And did they play cards together? Who played cards?
Deborah: My grandmother did. My grandmother would play pinochle with her.
Krista: And that's a hard game to play. So, she's just showing me the card-playing.
Deborah: Yeah, she was a serious player.
Krista: You have questions.
Deborah: Yeah, I guess I want to know if she was in any pain when she passed.
Krista: Please know that she left before she left, like when you thought she couldn't hear you. [Talking about the coma] I actually get this a lot, and I know what a blessing it is. The pain was here, in trying to fight to live; that was the pain. And she said, *"It just all went away."* And would you recognize that Jesus spoke to her before she crossed?
Deborah: I can see that, because the last person she talked to before she went into a coma was her preacher. [Joyful tears]
Krista: Well, she says that He spoke to her.
Deborah: Is her mother with her?
Krista: Yes. Your grandmother has swollen ankles. Did she have diabetes?
Deborah: Yeah. [Excited]
Krista: That's swollen ankles to me; that's how I see diabetes. She is with her. And was your grandmother the one that baked? And everything was made from scratch.
Deborah: Yes! [Excited]
Krista: And yes, of course she is. It's like, *"Of course!"* And did your grandmother and mother not see eye to eye all time?
Deborah: No, they didn't.
Krista: So recognize they still keep their personality [They were still bickering]. Your grandmother was bigger than your mother.
Deborah: Yes.
Krista: I almost feel like maybe German kind of big.
Deborah: Yeah, she was big, and my grandma's sister was huge.
Krista: And do you recognize that you brought her so much joy? Were you her favorite?
Deborah: I was her only.

Krista: You were her only, okay . . . that'll do it. You brought her so much joy. She was not a cat person, was she? Like, not at all!
Deborah: No! [Laughing]
Krista: But you got cats. [Indicating that she got them later]
Deborah: Afterwards, yeah.
Krista: Well, she ain't a cat person! It's so funny because she is talking about how much joy you brought to her; and she is just showing me the two of you together. She is joking and it's almost like I want to say, *"You turned out perfect . . . except for those cats!"* I mean she *really* had her issues with cats.
Deborah: Yeah, she was superstitious.
Krista: She did this when one walked in front of the car? [Indicate drawing an X across the windshield]
Deborah: [Laughing] Yeah, and she would just flip out if she saw a solid black cat, or people walking under ladders; just all of that, she would just flip out.
Krista: What was with her eyes? Because I just see these sparkly, sparkly eyes?
Deborah: They were like brownish but not brown, almost like hazel, light, real beautiful eyes. She had beautiful eyes. Does she see me? Does she see everyone and what they're doing?
Krista: She sees everyone . . . she sees everything! And I have a question. Was she not with you when your first daughter was born? Because I got that you missed her in the delivery room and I didn't know if it was with the first one or the second one.
Deborah: No, actually she had passed away February 25th and I had Kyle November 4th. She had been gone a week when I found out I was going to have Kyle.
Krista: Okay. You wanted her there; you really, really wanted her. **Deborah:** Yes.
Krista: Did you have your husband there that day?
Deborah: Yes.
Krista: And she's telling me that you would have been fine to just kick him out and take her.
Deborah: Yeah. [Laughing]
Krista: And if she was there, she would have done it. [Laughing] Which one of your daughters struggles with handwriting? It's like it's not even legible?
Deborah: Well, Holly struggles with the handwriting and she's got reading issues.

Krista: Does she mix up letters, or . . . ?
Deborah: Yeah.
Krista: Has there been questions about if she's got dyslexia or something like that?
Deborah: Yeah.
Krista: Because she is showing me that, and wants you to know she doesn't have a learning disability with that. Because I just got that it was illegible. So it's what she's reading, not just what she's writing. And she says not to let them put her on any drugs, and that it can be fixed.
Deborah: Nicole is on medication, the oldest one for ADHD.
Krista: Yeah. She doesn't like that stuff, but that's okay.
Deborah: Well yeah, because she didn't even want Tylenol.
Krista: She says, *"It's just kids not listening."* Her concern is that they're going to want to do the same thing with the younger one.
Deborah: Yeah, okay.
Krista: And she doesn't think that they need it, but she has an aversion to all that stuff anyway. Did someone need speech therapy or something? Or did they not enunciate right?
Deborah: That's my niece, Dailey, but that would be John's family. It's with my current husband, yeah.
Krista: Yeah but he's still associated with you.
Deborah: Yeah. She had to get speech therapy.
Krista: Is it your mother or your grandmother that wore an apron?
Deborah: My grandmother.
Krista: Did you have to pull yourself out of a depression? Because the grandmother is showing me that she was watching that.
Deborah: Yeah.
Krista: Did you take medication for that?
Deborah: I did.
Krista: Are you starting to feel like you're coming back into that again? [Into the depression]
Deborah: The last few days I've been really down due to Kyle's behavior and my oldest one, the one with ADHD. And my husband and her bashing heads because that's her stepdad.
Krista: Well, you know he's got control issues . . . and your daughter is difficult.

Deborah: Very! As sweet as she can be, but a real handful!
Krista: She said, *"You just have to be stern."* And I don't feel like it's just with your daughter; I feel like it's with your husband too. I can't use any other word and I feel like "stern" would be a word that she would use.
Deborah: Yeah.
Krista: She also says, *"You light up a room!"* You know that, don't you?
Deborah: She used to always tell me that.
Krista: Yeah, you do, and you don't have to succumb to that [Issues with her husband] because you're magnetic and your laughter is infectious. It's like she's telling you to be stern and remember how great you are. She says that what you're feeling will pass and that you don't need to go back to the medication. She says that you will get through it . . . you really will. Did your daughter have trouble in school?
Deborah: She did.
Krista: Did they think about holding her back?
Deborah: Yeah.
Krista: But they didn't, correct?
Deborah: Right.
Krista: Is it math?
Deborah: Yes, with her, but with Kyle, probably it's reading.
Krista: Do you not work?
Deborah: No.
Krista: Okay. So your husband makes all the money?
Deborah: That's correct.
Krista: Because she said, *"You can get a tutor, and he can afford it."* But he wouldn't want to, would he?
Deborah: No.
Krista: But, the kids come first.
Deborah: Yeah. And that's the way it is, and that's the way she was; the kids do come first.
Krista: Right. Math is still going to be a struggle and she says that you need to get her a tutor, but the other one will work out fine (without tutoring).
Deborah: Okay.
Krista: Any more question?

Deborah: Is Kyle going to be okay? I think that's my biggest thing. She's having a lot of problems.
Krista: Yes. Is she bullied or is she the bully? No, she's bullied.
Deborah: She's bullied, yeah.
Krista: She will (be okay). It's a tough age.
Deborah: Yeah.
Krista: *"It's a tough age."* I don't even know what her age is. I don't know which one is which, but your mom says, *"It's a tough age."*
Deborah: She's a pre-teen.
Krista: I don't know which one we're talking about here. But do you recognize that she needs more time with you?
Deborah: Yeah. I don't really know how to . . . it's hard to break them up and get time just one-on-one.
Krista: That's what she needs.
Deborah: Okay.
Krista: Is this the oldest one?
Deborah: Yeah.
Krista: Does she have a jealously over her sister?
Deborah: Oh gosh, yes!
Krista: She needs one-on-one with you. But you spoil her a little bit, don't you?
Deborah: Yeah. [Laughing]
Krista: So, you have to learn to use the things that you would spoil her with as reward. (Instead of just giving them)
Deborah: Okay.
Krista: Does she not think that she's a good girl? Let her know how great she is and tell her that her grandmother loves her. You have pictures of her, don't you? (Grandma)
Deborah: I have.
Krista: And your kids know by the pictures that it's grandma.
Deborah: Yeah, I keep pictures at my house on display. Does she like Suzy? (Dad's new wife)
Krista: *"She is okay."* That's what she said. She knows why he remarried. She said, *"She's not bad."*

Deborah: She's better than all the other ones.
Krista: She's good for your dad. Does she help keep him together?
Deborah: She keeps him calm, yeah. Dad was a very wild, very headstrong individual. I grew up in a really, really strict diehard Southern Baptist home. I mean my dad did let me go to couple of dances, but it was bad! Suzy tends to get on to him when he gets on to the girls, because dad has a really short fuse and he does not accept anything.
Krista: Don't argue!
Deborah: Exactly! You don't argue with him; you do as you are told. And she's always like, "Oh no, no, it's fine, now you calm down" kind of thing. Suzy's kind of keeping him together, I guess. After he got sick though, he really got better. He was not as hard as he was before. I even joked with my dad about how I wish he would have been more like this when I was young. He still gets like that sometimes, but he's not wound up as tight as he used to be.
Krista: Are you concerned about his health?
Deborah: I *stay* concerned about his health.
Krista: Has he had a checkup recently?
Deborah: Yeah.
Krista: Don't let him neglect that, because he would.
Deborah: Yeah, if I don't go and stand on him, he does.
Krista: He would, so make sure you stay on him with that, okay? And I'm not trying to freak you out like he's going to die – that's not what I mean, but stay on that. And make sure that in terms of cardiac, he's okay. I don't know if there's some lineage with that, just don't let him ignore his health. There's no reason to worry, just make sure you keep on him. He's not sick, that's not what I'm trying to say, so don't misconstrue that.
Deborah: Okay.

You just can't make this stuff up!

Chapter 15
5x7 Sideways, on the Shelf

Krista: As soon as you came on the line, I was told that you are missing someone . . . and I kept getting husband. Is this who are you missing?
Michelle: My husband, yes. [Crying]
Krista: I want to tell you that I am not going to hold you to a specific amount of time. So if we go over, that's no problem because I feel like there is something that's going to come out that you have to hear tonight. Okay?
Michelle: Okay.
Krista: We're going to talk about the husband. So that's what was ripped away from you.
Michelle: Mmm-hmm. He passed away a year ago in August.
Krista: That was the rug that was "ripped from under you" that we talked about when you called to schedule this reading, correct?
Michelle: Mmm-hmm.
Krista: Okay. We also have to talk about your mother. But first, who had heartburn or reflux, or something to that effect? Was that your husband?
Michelle: Yes! [Very surprised]
Krista: Okay. And did he have something with his neck? Because I want to hold my neck.
Michelle: Yeah.
Krista: And I feel like there is a mother in Spirit. Is that your mother or his?
Michelle: His.
Krista: Is there a necklace that you have of your mother's or your husband's? Because, I cannot let go of my neck. Did he buy you a necklace? Is there a necklace that you have?

Michelle: The only thing I can think of is I bought him a necklace for his birthday, about two months before he passed away.

Krista: Okay so there is the necklace! He loves that necklace! I feel like it fell right on the collar bone area.

Michelle: Mmm-hmm.

Krista: Now, what do you need to communicate with your mother? Are you not communicating with your mother?

Michelle: No, we do not talk.

Krista: Okay, so that's why he's telling me that you need to communicate with your mother!

Michelle: Mmm-hmm.

Krista: Do you guys have some kind of an anniversary or something that just recently passed?

Michelle: [Crying] We just had our wedding anniversary.

Krista: Why do I feel like he shouldn't have died? Do you understand that? I don't know if it was just soon, or if it kind of came out of nowhere; but I feel like it shouldn't have happened this way.

Michelle: [Crying] It did come out of nowhere, and he was only thirty-seven when he passed away.

Krista: Yeah, that would definitely be it then. Did he stay out of your business in regards to your mother, like he didn't interfere much?

Michelle: Yeah, he was pretty neutral about it.

Krista: Please understand, Michelle, that from the moment that you cross, you see things more clearly. It makes no difference what your life was like on earth; from the moment you ascend, you see things in a way you never have before. It's almost like he is getting choked up over it and he wants to say, *"I know I haven't been involved in this, but you really need to communicate things to your mother."* You have never sat down and really told her how you feel.

Michelle: No, no.

Krista: I feel like she has hurt you.

Michelle: Mmm-hmm.

Krista: I don't know how or why, but from this perspective it's not important that I do. But I feel like you've never really expressed to her what this has done to you. Do you understand this?

Michelle: Mmm-Hmm. Yes.

Krista: Do you even know how she's doing?

Michelle: No, not really.

Krista: You know how to contact her, correct?

Michelle: Mmm-hmm, yes.

Krista: Okay. Oh Lord, give me the words for this please! Life is too short. Life is *really* too short . . . and nobody knows that better than he does.

Michelle: Mmm-hmm.

Krista: I feel like you really hurt over your mom, but you don't deal with it. It's like you just kind of stuff it away. I feel like there is a lot of forgiveness that needs to take place in that relationship. And he is encouraging you to do this. He just keeps saying, *"Life is too short. Life is too short."* I don't know if your mom might have some kind of cardiac issue or something going on. I don't know what that means but every time he says life is just too short, I am drawn immediately to my chest and I feel this crushing in the middle of my chest. I don't know what's going on with your mother, but know that there is nothing that cannot be forgiven, okay?

Michelle: Mmm-hmm.

Krista: I know that he never pushed it . . . but he is pushing it now.

Michelle: Right.

Krista: There is a different understanding once you are there. I know you've had a whole year of struggle and uncertainty, and I feel like right when you kind of get on the brink of dealing with something and right when you feel like you're in a better place, something happens to pull you back. Do you understand this?

Michelle: Yes, very much!

Krista: Well, I have to tell you that I have got good news for you! Are you having struggles and uncertainties about finances?

Michelle: Yes.

Krista: What is the financial opportunity that you have coming up? Or do you realize you have a financial opportunity coming up for you? Because this is part of the good news.

Michelle: Possibly. I am looking into selling the house and finding something cheaper, which would probably save me a whole lot of money.

Krista: It'd be a relief.

Michelle: Yes.
Krista: I have to give you that I feel like you'll have positive change in the area of finance in about six months, okay?
Michelle: Oh okay!
Krista: I know that's longer than you wanted to go with it
Michelle: Right, yes.
Krista: Are you struggling with selling the house because of him?
Michelle: Not really. That's kind of a catch twenty-two question because my mind has not been in the right place because of his death. Not in the right place for me to be able to get things together and put it on the market.
Krista: I feel like you are going to reach a point where you go, "I am leaving behind these hard memories, this space." Please know that he is not in that stuff, okay? It doesn't matter where you go. He is going to be with you, okay?
Michelle: Mmm-hmm. Okay. [Crying]
His sickness just came on all of the sudden and he was sick for thirteen months . . . and then, he just passed away. He disappeared so he was basically "ripped away." It just happened so fast.
Krista: Was there something wrong in his stomach?
Michelle: Yes.
Krista: I don't know if this is him, or if this is you, but who was thinking, "We should have seen the connection." The connection between the acid reflux and the stomach (illness)? There was a connection, wasn't there?
Michelle: Yes. Right.
Krista: What are you wanting to change around your work?
Michelle: I want to improve my performance at work because I have just not been able to focus that well over the past year, and it just caused some things that shouldn't have happened. But it was just . . . I just couldn't get myself together.
Krista: Because it was like a part of you went when he left.
Michelle: Right!
Krista: Did you not celebrate the holidays last year? Or were you just not there, mentally? Because I feel like you're kind of dreading the holidays. But you are better than you were last year.

Michelle: Last year I think I was just kind of numb. I don't know . . . it's hard to describe.
Krista: Like you weren't really there; just going to the motions type of thing.
Michelle: Yeah. Yes, like I wasn't really feeling the full effect of his death.
Krista: Okay, but now you are.
Michelle: Yes, definitely.
Krista: And now it's like, "Oh my God! What do I do? How do I go on?"
Michelle: [Crying] Yeah.
Krista: And it's almost like you're still trying to learn how to function from day to day.
Michelle: Yeah, that's it exactly! Yeah.
Krista: You have done counseling, but it has not helped.
Michelle: Yes I have. Mmm-hmm. I don't think that grief counseling really helped me.
Krista: Have you gone into a depression?
Michelle: Yeah. I think I had.
Krista: In and out, in and out.
Michelle: Yes!
Krista: And it's almost like once you realize, "Oh my God! I'm in it!" Then you kind of step out . . . but you never really fully come out of it.
Michelle: Yeah, yeah that's very true.
Krista: I am feeling his symptoms so strongly. You cared for him when he was sick.
Michelle: Yes, I cared for him when he was sick.
Krista: He was at home the whole time, right up until the end.
Michelle: Yeah, he passed away at home. [Crying]
Krista: Because I'm seeing you with him. It's at home and it feels like this is right there towards the end.
Michelle: Mmm-hmm.
Krista: He says, *"I miss you too."*
Michelle: [Crying] Mmm-hmm.
Krista: He was your Soul-mate.
Michelle: Mmm-hmm. Yeah. [Crying]

Krista: He was a funny guy, was he not?

Michelle: Oh yeah! [Laughing]

Krista: Because it's almost like he wants to use an innuendo to say something cute to you. And I'm trying to figure out what it is he's trying to say. But that was kind of the way he talked to you, saying cute, funny stuff.

Michelle: Yes, it was.

Krista: Know that this is him coming through in his true character, in the way that you know him, okay?

Michelle: Mmm-hmm.

Krista: And he is just blowing you these kisses and it doesn't matter if he actually blew kisses in life, because that is *my* symbol for just this amazing love!

Michelle: Mmm-hmm.

Krista: And he says, *"You are still so beautiful!"* I don't know if he used to call you beautiful all the time, but he said, *"You are still so beautiful!"*

Michelle: Oh my gosh. [Crying]

Krista: And I'm supposed to tell you, *"I was there with her."* When was it that you thought you felt him? Because he is saying, *"I **was** there with her."* Notice where the emphasis is. So, when was the time you thought, "Wow! I could even feel him!"

Michelle: [Crying] Last Christmas, the holidays.

Krista: Did you put something special on the tree for him? Or put some kind of special thing up for him . . . *just* for him?

Michelle: Yes. I put his stocking up last year.

Krista: So, know that he is showing me that, okay? And it was *just* for him. And you have pictures up of him and of the two of you correct?

Michelle: Mmm-hmm, yes.

Krista: Okay. What is the one . . . it feels like it's taken sideways. It's a five by seven, and it's sideways. And is it just you or the two of you together? Do you know which one I'm talking about? And it sits on a shelf. Which one is that?

Michelle: Oh gosh! [Crying]

Krista: And I don't know if this was what you had there last year at Christmas, or if you have it there now, but know that he is showing me this photo. And is it in a metal frame? Is the frame light colored metal?

Michelle: The only frame I can think of was a picture of just me; it was in a white metal frame, in my wedding dress.
Krista: And that is five by seven, and sideways, right?
Michelle: Yes!
Krista: And where does that photo sit? Or where *did* that photo sit?
Michelle: He had it in his office. It used to be up on a shelf.
Krista: Up on the shelf okay. *"And could you please put that back there?"*
Michelle: Oh okay. [Laughing]
Krista: It's like he's not done looking at it.
Michelle: Wow! Really? [Chuckling]
Krista: Yes! And that was his thing. And he said, *"You don't know how many times I've looked at that."*
Michelle: Awe!
Krista: *"You are still just as beautiful."*
Michelle: Oh my gosh! Yes, he had my wedding photo in his office. It was in a white metal frame.
Krista: Yeah that's his favorite. He'd like to see that up . . . always.
Michelle: Okay. [Chuckling & crying]
Krista: And he says, *"I know that you think of me all the time and you miss me every day."* You dreamt of him last night, correct?
Michelle: [Crying] I think I had a dream about him last night. He was talking to me and it was so real, and I know I was talking in my sleep.
Krista: He *was* there with you; that was not a dream.
Michelle: I just kept hearing his voice. He was saying something to me; I don't know what he was saying.
Krista: *"I love you and I am here with you. You're not getting rid of me that easy!"* And that's his character, isn't it?
Michelle: Mmm-hmm, yeah.
Krista: He is not going anywhere, okay? And he says, *"You're going live to be an old lady. You don't want to hear that, but you are."*
Michelle: [Laughing] No.
Krista: You are, and I know you don't want that. Many other times you didn't know if you wanted to live it all, and he says, *"You're going to live to be an old lady . . .*

and I'm going to be with you every step of the way!" Is there anything you want to say to him?

Michelle: [Crying] I just love him and I miss him.

Krista: *"I know, I know. I am so sorry I left you. I never wanted to leave you."* And he says, *"I hope I was a good husband."*

Michelle: [Crying] Oh my gosh! I can't believe you just said that! He used to tell me that all the time. He was the *best* husband! He was such a good husband!

Krista: I don't know if you have said this, or if it's just gone through your mind, but he is telling me that your big thing was that you (as a couple) didn't even have a chance to live yet; like you had so many plans and so many dreams. Do you understand this?

Michelle: Yeah, oh yeah! We were together a total of seven years, married five; and I feel like we were just getting started.

Krista: Yeah.

Michelle: We talked about things that we were going to do.

Krista: Yeah. Did you want to buy a second home somewhere one day? Did you guys talk about that?

Michelle: Yeah, he and I had talked about buying another house.

Krista: He wants you to continue with your plans . . . and he says, *"I'll be right there with you. And would you please call your mother? Because she loves you too. I know she doesn't always show it, but she loves you. How could anyone not love you? You are wonderful!"* Wow! What is his first name, please?

Michelle: His first name is Kevin.

Krista: Does he not like his middle name? Because when you said, "Kevin," he said, *"Ask about the middle name."* Or does he like the middle name better than the first name? I don't know why I have to ask.

Michelle: He always loved his middle name because it was so different. He had his dad's middle name.

Krista: What is that?

Michelle: Hamilton.

Krista: And did he buy you flowers shortly before he passed? Or did you buy them for him? What were the flowers? It's was something special. I don't know if it was special to you or special to him. But he showed me these flowers.

Michelle: No, his mother bought flowers for our anniversary. Our five-year anniversary was August the 15th and he passed away on August the 28th.
Krista: Oh okay. Did you not think that he was really aware of the flowers? Because he is saying, *"Just tell her I loved the flowers."*
Michelle: Oh gosh! [Surprised and crying]
Krista: Did you think at the time that he didn't even acknowledge the flowers, or doesn't know the flowers were here, or whatever?
Michelle: Is it maybe the flowers I picked out for his memorial?
Krista: Which ones have yellow? I am feeling like they're yellow; I think they are lilies with the long, thin things in the mix. It was the flowers for an occasion.
Michelle: Yeah I believe it was yellow lilies in the arrangement that his mom bought us.
Krista: They are so present with him and the biggest reason it was so special was because that was your anniversary.
Michelle: Mmm-hmm. That was our last anniversary.
Krista: And he says, *"You will always be my wife, my Soul-mate, my love."* Did he used to call you "Love?"
Michelle: Yeah. Mmm-hmm. Yeah he used to call me "Love."
Krista: Okay . . . *"and you are!"* After I turn the recording off, I am going to give you the name of a gentleman for some counseling, okay? I just intuitively feel that he would be really good for you.
Michelle: Mmm-hmm.
Krista: I hope that you got what you needed here tonight with this reading. And I hope that it was everything you wanted it to be . . . and then some.
Michelle: Yeah, but I wasn't expecting this kind of reading, actually. [She was expecting a psychic reading and never expected her husband to come through]
Krista: Have you never had this kind of reading?
Michelle: No.
Krista: This is what I do. And there's usually a lot of detail, a lot of things like you got here tonight. My readings are not about giving out winning lottery numbers; they're about emotional healing. That's what my work is. And even though it wasn't what you expected, I know it's what you needed . . . and I just hope that you realize that.

Michelle: I did because I have not healed yet; I have had the hardest time struggling since he passed away.
Krista: Yeah.
Michelle: I really have, but now I feel like a lot has been lifted off my shoulders.
Krista: Good, that's good. And he says, *"That's what I'm here for."*
Michelle: Is he with me a lot?
Krista: Yes, yes he is.

In summary, within just a few short months, Michelle sold her house and was able to reduce her expenses, just like we talked about.

You just can't make this stuff up!

Chapter 16
Show Me the Money!

Krista: Hi Leslie. I know you're looking to connect with someone specific, but I can't guarantee who comes through and who doesn't. Typically, if there's someone that you're looking for specifically, you can call for them and they will come through, though not always.
Krista: I don't know if this is your anxiety that I'm feeling. It might just be a feeling of being anxious. So I'm going to ask that you try to relax and not be anxious.
Leslie: Okay.
Krista: Is your mother in Spirit, Leslie?
Leslie: Yes.
Krista: Okay. I am scratching the side of my face and I don't know why I'm doing that, but I'm not going to be able to stop until I can place this.
Leslie: She used to rub the side of her nose.
Krista: No, this is the side of my face. I feel like there's something here. Did she have oxygen going into her nose, and the tubes across the face?
Leslie: No. My dad passed over and he used oxygen when he was sitting and reading a lot during the day, so he would've had a tube.
Krista: Okay, your dad. He passed before your mother, correct?
Leslie: No, no. My mother passed away before. My mother passed years about seventeen years before my dad, but my stepmother just passed.
Krista: Okay. [This is the woman I was feeling] You're probably going to have a lot people come through. I'm just trying to place who we have here with us.

Leslie: I don't know the circumstances about my stepmother. She just passed very recently and she was in the hospital for very, very short time, so I can't tell you what all went on with her.
Krista: Or if she has something in her nose.
Leslie: Yeah, I have no idea.
Krista: Okay. Who wore glasses or wore glasses when they read?
Leslie: [Laughing] That would be all of them, actually; all three of them would have worn glasses to read.
Krista: Okay. I'm going to try to figure out who this is, because at this point I'm not seeing; I'm just feeling, I'm getting impressions.
Leslie: Well, tell me the impressions because if it's any one of those three, I can sort it out myself. I expected to hopefully hear from all three of them, so I can sort out who is who if you just tell me what's going on.
Krista: Okay. And sometimes so many people come through it's like a stadium of people.
Leslie: Right.
Krista: I'm itching everywhere! So who is it who might have had allergies or skin conditions?
Leslie: I guess my stepmother. If any of them, she would be the only one really, I guess, and she just passed.
Krista: Okay. Did someone have some type of a surgery in their chest? Or they have something happen with their chest?
Leslie: Yeah, Jackie, my stepmother did. She's the one that just passed. So what does she want to say or tell me, or whatever?
Krista: I don't know yet. I'm trying to let her finish giving me everything that she wants to give me. Right now, I'm getting her afflictions. I don't know what her surgery was, if it was heart surgery or what, but she said it was the drugs that made her itch. It was very specific on my chest, almost like how you itch when you have a scar or when something's healing, or something along those lines.
Leslie: Okay.
Krista: Okay, it is Ms. Jackie that we have here. She has *just* passed. She's bringing someone else through.
Leslie: Yes. My dad, probably.

Krista: Okay. Well, he's saying that he's the one who brought her through. [Laughing]
Leslie: Yeah, that makes sense.
Krista: So, yes, he brought her through . . . it's like this is so fresh that it's a little difficult to communicate.
Leslie: Right.
Krista: When people pass, they have to learn to communicate with us. They can't just hop right in, and there are always people that come and help them; they show them how to communicate with us.
Leslie: And dad's communicated with me before; he's communicated with me in dreams. Okay, so what does he want to say?
Krista: What is his first name please?
Leslie: Ian.
Krista: [Choking] Did Ian have a condition where he choked, or he couldn't breathe or something?
Leslie: Yeah.
Krista: They do that (show me their afflictions) so that you're clear with whom it is we're talking to.
Leslie: Yes. I am clear! [Getting frustrated] But I want to know what they want to say. I'm really anxious!
Krista: I know.
Leslie: I have anxiety. I'm anxious and I want to get answers to questions. We have established who they are. I knew they would be the people who would come through. My mother might come through too, and my ex-husband might come through, but I know them. It's okay, so just tell me! Don't try to identify them anymore!
Krista: Okay, Leslie, this is how I work! And when you have anxiety and when you try to push faster than I can receive, it makes it very difficult. I want to make sure that the messages that I give you are clear, so that you clearly understand what they're trying to tell you. And when you push me faster than they can get it to me and faster than I can process it, it makes it very, very difficult! Okay? So I understand your anxiety; I feel it in my body. So let me just ask Ian here. [Pausing for a moment] He's saying that you have been through a lot of . . . and his word is "turmoil." Is this recent? Or is this a long time ago?

Leslie: Both.
Krista: Both okay. Who drank in your family when you were a child, when you were growing up?
Leslie: Oh he did! They all did, but he did a lot!
Krista: Okay. Because when he's talking about your turmoil, he says that it started with the drinking, and he is showing me that it was back when you were young, okay?
Leslie: Okay.
Krista: He's saying, *"I wasn't always there for her."*
Leslie: No, he wasn't always there.
Krista: And you felt very alone a lot, and he says that you felt like you didn't have anywhere to turn. But I get the sense that it was not just then, that this has been a pattern in your life.
Leslie: Right. Yes.
Krista: That feeling that people aren't there for you.
Leslie: Yeah.
Krista: And he says, *"These aren't words I would normally use, but I'm really sorry."* Do you understand that he wasn't good at saying he's sorry?
Leslie: Yes, I understand. [Laughing] I know that very well.
Krista: He said that he didn't have accountability. He was a smart man, but he didn't know . . .
Leslie: [Interrupts] Right he is.
Krista: It feels like he was educated, book smart, but not a lot of common sense.
Leslie: He was smart. He had a good IQ and he was well educated, but he didn't have accountability.
Krista: Was he the philanderer? Or was it your mother? Because it's like there were issues there with fidelity.
Leslie: Yeah, we all tie together. My father was, ultimately; he was the philanderer, but there were issues with them.
Krista: Yeah, it was like a perpetuating thing. That's what he's showing me.
Leslie: Yes, yes.
Krista: Would you recognize that your stepmother saved him?
Leslie: I suppose, yeah. I'll give him that. [A little sarcastic]
Krista: You didn't want to hear that.

Leslie: No, I'll give him that; whatever, yes, no, that's fine. He was cruel to my mother, but that's okay if my stepmother saved him, fine.
Krista: He was; he was cruel.
Leslie: But what I want to know is what's going to happen now? That's what I want to know! [Still frustrated] Now that they have all passed and it's left up to us and it's a big mess; what's going to happen? That's what I want to know from him, since he set it all up!
Krista: Oh my word! This is funny because you get this from him; he says, *"Straight in and out – right to the point!"*
Leslie: That's right! Impatience . . . let's get on with it. What the hell are you trying to tell me? Because he made things very tough; he muddied the waters. If he could stir things up and make them more difficult; he always did! So now I want to know what he's going to do for me at the end, with all this mess.
Krista: He hears your question. Let me just process what he's saying.
Leslie: [Laughing] I bet he does!
Krista: [Laughing] You know, they can read your thoughts too, by the way.
Leslie: Yeah, well, he has read a lot lately. I mean, I appreciate that everything went the way it did in the end and all. But now, here we are; we're left and they've all escaped!
Krista: I don't know how many brothers or sisters you have, but he says, *"It's like they're all running amok, just trying to get to it all!"*
Leslie: Yeah, no kidding!
Krista: What does that mean "get to it all?" Do you know what that means?
Leslie: Yeah. Because there is stuff that has to be sorted out and I have two stepsisters and a stepbrother; and the stepbrother has already big time cheated!
Krista: He's come in and taken over, yeah.
Leslie: Oh no, not "come in and taken over," just conned his way into a brand new car and a brand new TV and just taken them! And nobody even knew about it. And he's already conned my stepmother into putting his name on them before she passed.
Krista: So when he says "taken over," he means taking over parts of the estate?
Leslie: He's stolen things, he's legally stolen things, and now my stepsister is in charge of it all. And she's too limited, she's too "by the book" and she's older and she just wants to get it done. She will let him slide with more stuff and that

worries me; my younger sister is fine with whatever. I'm the one who's going to really be pissed off and stir the pot constantly! [Very angry now]

Krista: Okay.

Leslie: There's a lawyer I don't trust and an accountant I don't trust, and yeah it's going to be a mess and I'm really pissed about the whole thing! I want to know the bottom line! How bad is it going to be for me? Because I have always assumed that there would be something, and I'm beginning to really wonder once they all get through muddying the waters and screwing around.

Krista: I'm sorry. I'm just telling you that I'm starting to take on your anxiety again, so just take a deep breath. Let's just relax a little bit. [Taking a moment to relax, while Ian speaks to me]

Krista: How do I say this? I asked for another way to say that and the answer that I got was, *"Bullshit! Just say it."*

Leslie: [Laughing] Yeah, good. Then just say it.

Krista: He said that nobody's ever going to be happy, and then he said, *"The story of my life."*

Leslie: [Laughing] That's a copout on his part! That's a copout, Dad, sorry but I don't believe you. Oh dear! So, I'm going to get screwed, basically.

Krista: Well that's the way he feels (that no one will be happy). It's my experience that when people pass, they don't lie, so to him, that's true; that's the truth, as he knows it. Wow, he had a temper!

Leslie: Oh did he ever! Instant temper . . . and I'm not far behind him.

Krista: No, you're not! Okay, we're going to find a more loving way to approach this . . .

Leslie: [Laughing] It's okay. I can take it; I'm used to him.

Krista: I have only ever come across one person who was angry, but I think that your impatience is kind of stirring things up a little bit for him.

Leslie: [Laughing] Which is good, because we always went round and round. He told me to f*ck off one time and then he said, "No, but you're my daughter, so whatever." That's what our relationship has been like.

Krista: Yes. And his answer is, *"If I had known all this, I'd have just burned it all up!"*

Leslie: Yeah, well you could have just shared a little bit; that would have been nice, that's what I always wanted. That was too easy; he never could share.

Krista: Did he drink everything away? Or piss it away? It's like it was always "for him."

Leslie: He was always too busy with himself, yeah. It was all for him and he was too busy with important things. He didn't have time to share it because he was all tied up and he managed to tie things up and screw things up and muddy the waters endlessly, so that there was very little he could share. His father shared everything and that's what I think is very funny. His father shared it, and then when he got it, he couldn't quite reach to share . . . and now we are at the other end and I'm in the worst situation of everybody!

Krista: He struggled his whole life.

Leslie: No, he didn't struggle at all. He didn't, although there was always somebody there to pay the bills.

Krista: No, I meant emotionally.

Leslie: Okay that's fine, but physically, his needs were always taken care of; there was always somebody to pay the bills and that pisses me off because that's the thing I have never had!

Krista: Right, right.

Leslie: I struggled to pay the bills. He's a pr*ck and I will punch him in the nose when I finally see him! I have to because he just made me so unhappy for so long! I get the message from you, basically I'm screwed and I'm going to be screwed, and the thing that I thought was going to happen is going to.

Krista: No, no, no! It's interesting, Leslie, because he's saying that the apple doesn't fall far from the tree. Did he raise your stepbrother?

Leslie: Oh everybody's known everybody our whole lives; it's very complicated for me to go any further than that.

Krista: So he was an influence on your stepbrother?

Leslie: Oh yeah! Oh yeah!

Krista: Okay, because what he's telling me . . . great, now *he's* impatient! When he says, *"The apple doesn't fall far from the tree,"* he's actually talking about you *and* the stepbrother.

Leslie: Great. So I should understand his evil ways because I'm like that too? Okay.

Krista: That's not what he's saying! He's talking about impatient, straight-forward, matter-of-fact, no room for the warm and fuzzies.

Leslie: Yeah. Except that my stepbrother isn't trustworthy; you can't trust him one percent . . . ever! You could never trust him.
Krista: He said that the one who is taking care of it was the best one for it because she's got a good heart.
Leslie: Yes, that's good. Okay that's good.
Krista: Do you understand that?
Leslie: That's good. Yes, I do understand that. He asked me to do it, and I said "No." I said no because he wasn't local.
Krista: He does say that she will not . . .
Leslie: [Interrupts] She's not going to take charge and be aggressive enough, but she's got the biggest heart, so that's fine, that's fine. He asked me to do it and I said no because I don't live there. It would be much more difficult for me.
Krista: He said that she's going to be fair. He said that things were never fair.
Leslie: No, they weren't.
Krista: But she will be fair.
Leslie: Well, that's good. I hope she will.
Krista: She will be fair *to you*, do you understand?
Leslie: Good. Yeah.
Krista: Were you considered like the "black sheep" of the kids? Or were you like the one that was . . .
Leslie: [Interrupts] I was! All right, let me tell you: I was his daughter; all three of the other children were not his children, okay?
Krista: Okay.
Leslie: And to make things fair, he always slighted me, so he wouldn't play favorites . . . but he ended up playing favorites a lot, so it's all very convoluted and I don't want to get into it. But we all know exactly what went on and what didn't go on! So I just want to know going forward, how well it's going to come out? Because man, I feel like I have been shafted big time!
Krista: This is why I asked if you were the black sheep, because out of all of them, she is the one who will be fair *to you*, okay?
Leslie: Okay.
Krista: That's the first thing.
Leslie: Oh it's good. [Softening a bit]

Krista: And he said, *"I have never been fair to you..."*
Leslie: [Laughing] Okay thanks. Yes, that's true.
Krista: Oh boy! Was your husband never fair to you either? Because he says, *"Like all of the other men in your life."*
Leslie: Yep!
Krista: *"It all started with me."*
Leslie: That's right, and that's correct!
Krista: Is she the baby of the family? Or would . . .
Leslie: No she's the oldest. I was just going to tell you there was little joke for years. And most of his life, he was under the impression that Nancy (the oldest daughter who is in charge of everything) was his daughter.
Krista: Right.
Leslie: And she could have been, but she was not. But it was allowed to perpetuate all through her life; he was allowed to think that he was her father. And we didn't find out until he crossed that it was not true, but it could have been true because he was a philanderer, and so that tied everybody together.
Krista: Okay, that makes sense, okay.
Leslie: Yes.
Krista: All right. Okay, out of the bunch of them . . . Why is he calling them, "the bunch of them?"
Leslie: Yeah that's true, that's true. The youngest one, Barbara and I were always close and we're close now again, and I think I can trust her. Does he think I can trust her?
Krista: Yes. Yes. Because he mentioned "the baby," he called her "the baby."
Leslie: Yeah, Barbara is the baby. She and I are good friends and I think she's as honest as I am. We are straight down the line and this is the way it is.
Krista: But the one who is handling it, she is the diplomatic one of the bunch.
Leslie: Right. Right, she's the oldest and she's got the heart and all that, okay.
Krista: She does, and she will make sure that things are fair. Is there a piece of property that needs to be sold?
Leslie: Yes.
Krista: Okay. Who is this that wants to live in that house and does not want it sold? Like someone wants it for themselves.

Leslie: [Laughing] I don't know. It's probably Dick. It's probably the boy because he's such a crook! He would do fine if he takes that as his part, but he would do it in such a way that he'd cheat.
Krista: He said it's not going to happen, okay?
Leslie: Okay, it's not going to happen.
Krista: Did someone die intestate, without a will?
Leslie: No. Why?
Krista: Because it's like there was something that was missing from the will.
Leslie: I have no idea. Oh sh*t! What did they forget to do?
Krista: Okay. Let me just ask what this is, because I'm getting probate. Is this going through probate?
Leslie: Well it will be, because she just died.
Krista: Okay.
Leslie: The last of all of them just died. Now my generation is left, so it all will have to be dealt with.
Krista: Okay, so that makes sense. I'm from Florida, and in Florida, when you die intestate – without a will – it goes to probate. But you don't have to have lawyers involved in all that stuff if there is a will.
Leslie: This is Louisiana. We do in Louisiana and they've got wills and lawyers and everything!
Krista: The baby, she is the one who knows how to work the older one. Does that make sense?
Leslie: Oh yeah! Yes. Yeah Barbara knows how to work her, yes. She's already done it.
Krista: She does. And he says, *"It's going to be fair to all of you."* But he wants you to know it will be fair to *you*, okay?
Leslie: Okay.
Krista: It *will* be fair to you! Who is it that wanted the antiques? I don't know if it's true antiques, because I'm seeing that it's older furniture.
Leslie: I don't know and I don't care. The majority of the furniture was Jackie's, so it would go to any of the kids that would want it. It wouldn't be mine, so that's that. There were only a few things of my dad's that I wanted, and I think Dick took them one at a time when he would come to visit, because I have asked Nancy about it, and those were very few things that existed, most of them have

disappeared. So, I'm sure Dick conned my stepmother into giving him something more every time he came over to visit . . . until it was all gone.

Krista: Let me tell you something funny. Every time you use the word "Dick," he says, *"And he is."* [Laughing]

Leslie: [Laughing] Yes, he is! And the new wife called him Richard, and I said, "No it's Dick. He is a Dick!" Let me just tell you very quickly. He got my dad's car when my dad passed. And when Jackie went into the hospital, Nancy called him and he drove over from Texas to Louisiana in that car. And when he got there, she had just passed. Nancy told him that she passed and he left dad's car and took Jackie's brand new car – which he helped her pick out – and he drove away to Texas. And when Nancy came over the next day and discovered that the wrong car was gone, she was hysterical! And when she finally found the pink slip, from when he bought the car with her, she found that Jackie paid for it, but she put his name on it too . . . so it's his. So that's what kind of a dick, Dick is! [Laughing]

Krista: Is he the one that has never had to work for anything?

Leslie: Pretty much, yeah. Yeah. He pretty much didn't.

Krista: Okay. These are very important words that he wants you to know. *"It's all going to come out in the wash."*

Leslie: Oh good. I hope so!

Krista: It's all going to come out in the wash, okay? There is a piece of furniture; it feels like a bureau or a wardrobe or something. It's tall and dark and it's ornate; and I think it's like an antique and that's going to be his, okay? And he's going to pitch a fit, because he would rather have the money. [Laughing] He says that Dick doesn't see the value in anything.

Leslie: This is Dick? Dick is going to pitch a fit because there's a tall antique wardrobe that he's going to get that he doesn't want; he wants the money?

Krista: Yes, he wants the money.

Leslie: Okay.

Krista: He says, *"It's sentimental value."* I don't know who it should be sentimental to; it if it was to his mother, or if it should be sentimental to him. He says that he has it sorted out so that everything is equal.

Leslie: That's just it; I don't know. Well, that car should definitely count as part of Dick's.

Krista: It should.
Leslie: And Dick also bought two TV's for Jackie while he was visiting and took one for himself. And then, when she passed, he said, "I want the other one." But Nancy said, "No way!" He said, "Well, I need one upstairs." And she said, "I have got a kid who doesn't even have one." And I thought, "Well, f*ck him!" I said, "Cut him off. Don't let him have anything else. The car was a big mistake! He got the car and the TV; he's done, he's cut off!" But she's not that strict; she'll get conned.
Krista: She's going to operate from her heart, but recognize that the baby is going to be the one to . . .
Leslie: [Interrupts] Keep her straight.
Krista: Yeah. You're the wild card!
Leslie: I know I am. I know.
Krista: You're the wild card, but again, in fact, the apple doesn't fall far from the tree. You're the one who won't stand for injustice because you have had it your whole life and you won't tolerate it. It's very important that you know this; this is not something where this man will have to be sued, okay? It's not.
Leslie: That's good.
Krista: This is set to settle in within sixty days? [I don't think she ever really heard me say this]
Leslie: I have no idea what's going to happen. It sounds like there was such a mess that the lawyer and the accountant will milk it as far as they can, tracing it back so far and taking it all forward, and blah, blah, blah . . . it sounds like a real con!
Krista: And he says, *"Well, that's what they do. And you know that."*
Leslie: Yeah, I know. I know, but it sounds like they are conned.
Krista: And your dad didn't trust lawyers either. You know that, right?
Leslie: [Laughing] Yes, I know that.
Krista: And he didn't trust doctors.
Leslie: I know. I don't trust any of them either. And I don't trust men. So there we are; we've come to that point.
Krista: [Laughing] Right.
Leslie: Yes, I don't trust people in general, I'm afraid.
Krista: I understand, I understand.

Show Me The Money!

Leslie: Animals are better. I just want to know; in the near future, am I going to be strapped for money for a long time before this whole thing is settled? I'm really concerned about that.

Krista: He says that things happened that got you in over your head.

Leslie: I'm not in over my head, and I have kept my nose clean, because I was anticipating it being rough. I did some things that I had to do to the house to keep it straight. There's still a lot more to be done that I can't do.

Krista: Okay, so those were the unexpected expenses. It affected your finances, like you had to take it from your pocket to do them.

Leslie: Oh yeah, but I'm okay now. I'm straight. So going forward, he's saying there's not going to be anything. [I told you she wasn't listening]

Krista: No! He's telling me, *"In about sixty days."* I don't know if this is sixty days from when she died, or if it's sixty days from now. But he said in about sixty days, okay?

Leslie: Okay.

Krista: He says, *"Jesus Christ! She can't wait sixty days?"*

Leslie: Oh yes, I can! See, he never understood that I lived in the real world. His secretary use to say, "He never paid for anything. He thought that $50.00 is all he needed for the month, because I paid all the bills for the company." He never understood the real world, and I lived in the real world, always buying the milk and the gas and everything was accountable.

Krista: Right.

Leslie: That bastard! Saying, *"You can't wait sixty days!"* If it is sixty days, that's really nice, dad. Just tell me it's f*cking sixty days! He's such a pr*ck! Okay, so in sixty days I'll be okay?

Krista: He says, *"It's all going to come out in the wash in about sixty days."*

Leslie: Okay.

Krista: I don't know if it gets dispersed in that time, or if that means that it gets decided and you get word about it in that time.

Leslie: Okay.

Krista: But he says, *"By the spring, you'll be fine."*

Leslie: By the spring I'll be fine, okay. That's fine, if I know that. Jesus, that helps so much! It's an answer, and it's all I ever wanted from him.

Krista: He says you'll still hate Dick, though. [Laughing] That's been forever.
Leslie: Well that's understandable. Yeah that will never stop.
Krista: That's between you guys.
Leslie: He's got the same birthday that I do, and he's three years older and he puts a bad name on my birthday.
Krista: What's your birthday?
Leslie: November 29th. He's the same date, but he's three years older. [Laughing] Lenore (Astrologer) says he's all of the negative traits of a Sagittarian.
Krista: Oh yeah, I understand.
Leslie: So there we are, okay.
Krista: So he says, *"By spring. You'll be fine by spring."*
Leslie: Okay that's fine. I can live that long.
Krista: He gave this to the one with the biggest heart, who would be the most fair to the whole bunch. I don't know why I called y'all "the whole bunch." [Laughing]
Leslie: [Laughing] Yeah, well, because we think of each other that way. He says, "I've known them all my life. It is like a bunch."
Krista: Okay. Know that Barbara is your ally, okay?
Leslie: Okay.
Krista: Don't forget that.
Leslie: Good, good.
Krista: Do you recognize that she had more tolerance for him than most of them did?
Leslie: Oh yes, definitely! Yes, yes. Because she has a different temperament
Krista: So here is what he's saying; it's almost feels like a warning.
Leslie: Don't say too much because she's going to be pissed.
Krista: Yeah. You don't want you to piss her off, talking about how you feel about him, okay? Because she's your ally.
Leslie: Right, I know. I visited her once and let it rip, and she was upset and concerned and didn't agree with the half of it, and she didn't understand where I was coming from. So, yeah, I will have to tread softly on that.
Krista: Yes, but what he says is, *"You were right."* He said he knows he was a son of a bitch.
Leslie: [Laughing] Yeah, he was.

Krista: And he said, *"I tried to make it fair in the end."* He tried to make it fair because he knew what he was in life and he didn't want to be that in his death, okay?
Leslie: [Softening, somber] Yeah, okay.
Krista: Recognize that he's trying to heal these relationships.
Leslie: Okay.
Krista: He's finally trying to be accountable and he's trying to heal these relationships, and again, he says, *"I'm sorry."* He's sorry and he doesn't think that you'll take his apology. He says, *"You'll say okay, but you won't really take it to heart . . . but you can't be pissed off forever."*
Leslie: He's right, he's right. (About not taking the apology to heart) [Laughing]
Krista: I know.
Leslie: He's right.
Krista: But listen; this is more important than money, okay? He says, *"You can't be pissed off forever; it's no way to live. Take it from someone who knows."*
Leslie: [Crying] Yeah. Okay.
Krista: He doesn't want you to feel this way.
Leslie: [Still crying] So, does he have any idea of what I should do with the rest of my life, assuming I have a bit? You know, my mother was not even seventy-two when she died, and dad was almost eighty-nine. He lived seventeen years more than she did, and he was such a son of bitch, and she was such nice person.
Krista: I know. She was so wounded.
Leslie: Yeah, she was. I'm wondering how much longer I have. I'm concerned about that because I'm not that far from when my mother passed.
Krista: Okay, he said, *"You're not going to go any time soon."*

In summary, Leslie received the first of two very sizeable checks ***exactly*** sixty days after the date of this reading.

You just can't make this stuff up!

Chapter 17
How Much Money do You Need?

Krista: Jodi, I know you want to talk to your mom today, and I got this sense of her when she was young on the back of a motorcycle. It doesn't have to be literal; it could be like that "free Spirit" type of thing. [Jodi Laughs]
I don't mean it in a bad way; it's just that free Spirit energy. I feel like that's where you get it, from – your mom. That's where she was before responsibility came and made her grow up. Did she have children *right after* getting married? Because it feels like when responsibility came, it was done *to* her.
Jodi: I believe that she was pregnant with my brother when she got married.
Krista: Okay. That's what it feels like, but I didn't want to say it that way. [Laughing] I didn't want to say, "Shotgun wedding!" She really was a very, very free Spirit. Your dad would know this . . . but are his mental faculties not there right now? What's going on with him?
Jodi: He has had some issues with being overmedicated and things like that. And sometimes, getting confused and not knowing where he is at the time, that kind of thing. He's been better recently.
Krista: Do you have a trip planned to go see him in the next couple of months? [Holding up two fingers]
Jodi: Actually, in two weeks. A week from Saturday, I'll see him.
Krista: Okay. You do know that he lights up when you come. Do you realize that?
Jodi: No.
Krista: Are you the baby?
Jodi: Yes.
Krista: He's geographically closer to other family members, correct?
Jodi: Yes, closer to my sister, Leah.

Krista: Okay. Is she the serious one?
Jodi: Yes. [Laughing]
Krista: Because I was going to ask why is it that he doesn't light up with her, and I heard, *"Because she's no fun."*
Jodi: [Laughing] That would be true!
Krista: Did your dad teach you to play poker or blackjack when you were little?
Jodi: My mom taught us to play pinochle.
Krista: Okay. This feels like your dad doing "boy things" with you. Do you understand this?
Jodi: Kind of, yeah. When I was really young, he was in construction, so he would take me to the jobsite to ride the Caterpillars (Construction equipment), and stuff like that.
Krista: Does your mother have a birthday or anniversary coming up?
Jodi: [Surprised] Yeah, her birthday is in three days.
Krista: Okay. And that's why you wanted to make sure you got this reading; you wanted to make sure you contacted her.
Jodi: Yes.
Krista: Okay, because she says, *"Aren't you going to celebrate?"* You do celebrate, don't you?
Jodi: I do.
Krista: What is it that you do? Because it's like you acknowledge her every time.
Jodi: I don't know that it's anything specific, but it's just a day that I really pay attention.
Krista: Did you recently put flowers in your house? I see flowers around you. She says, *"They're lovely,"* and I don't know what flowers she's talking about.
Jodi: Probably the flowers we put on her grave for Mother's Day. (Just a few weeks ago)
Krista: You went there with both daughters, correct?
Jodi: Yes.
Krista: Okay. Was your mother arthritic? Or were her fingers crooked? Because I feel like my hands are really achy, especially in my knuckles.
Jodi: No, she had beautiful hands.
Krista: Do you have issues with your hands? It's like carpal tunnel or something.
Jodi: Yes. [Laughing]

How Much Money Do You Need?

Krista: Okay, so that's her way of showing you that she knows what you're going through, and what's going on with you. And she's thanking me for bringing up Mark. (From a previous reading) She's so glad you didn't go down that road. Were you considering it?
Jodi: [Laughing] Yeah.
Krista: And you stopped yourself in the nick of time!
Jodi: Yeah.
Krista: She says she's going to have to send you a good man.
Jodi: [Laughing] Please!
Krista: She says that she knew how to stick with them! Who is Dan or Daniel?
Jodi: I was once engaged to a man named Dan.
Krista: Okay. Why does she bring up that name when she says, "I'll send you a good one?" Did she like him, or not like him?
Jodi: Oh, I don't know that anyone in my family liked him. My sisters call those my "lost years."
Krista: She says, *"Well, we all have those."* I'm telling you, I really think your mother was a little bit of a wild child.
Jodi: [Laughing] Well, she always maintained, but it's like there was always an undercurrent.
Krista: It reminds me of that country song, "I Saw Momma before she was Momma." [Laughing] I'll have to send it to you; it's hilarious! She was a little bit of a hellion, and life settled her down. And life settled your sister down too . . . she just forgot to stop!
[Jodi Laughing]
Krista: Did you always think your sister was her favorite?
Jodi: Yeah, I pretty much thought everyone was her favorite, over me.
Krista: Do you realize now – or could you open yourself to accept – that the issues you had with your mom is that she saw so much of herself in you? Do you understand that?
Jodi: [Crying] Yeah.
Krista: No boundaries . . . and you trust everyone.
Jodi: [Laughing and crying] Yeah.
Krista: And you love everyone.
Jodi: Yes.

Krista: And you were on this constant adventure, and she was afraid for you because that's what she was like. And she said she had to grow up too soon. You wanted it; you wanted to settle down and grow up, didn't you?

Jodi: Mmm-hmm.

Krista: And if it were up to you, you would have been a stay-at-home mom all the time. And of course, you would still have to rule the world on the side. But it's like you just wanted to grow up so fast.

Jodi: [Crying] Mmm-hmm. She always told me to slow down. She always criticized that I was trying to grow up too fast, which I do to my daughter Lydia now, too. [Laughing]

Krista: Lydia is your youngest one?

Jodi: Yes.

Krista: Now recognize the pattern here. Her youngest one is just like her and you guys butted heads. Your youngest one is just like you, and you guys butt heads. And she said, *"You could only hope that she turns out half as wonderful as you!"* [Jodi crying and very touched]

She's really very, very proud of you! And I may have to be very delicate here. Do you recognize that your mom would just open her mouth and whatever flew out, flew out?

Jodi: Yeah, I mean she pretty much told it like it was. Yeah.

Krista: So, we're going to do that here, okay? She's very proud of you in how you turned out, and she always wondered which would reach maturation first, your brains or your boobs.

Jodi: [Laughing hysterically] Wow!

Krista: It's like you matured physically before you matured mentally. And she was so afraid for the longest time that, that part of you was going to rule you. And you did good . . . but you don't always have the greatest taste in men.

Jodi: Yeah, she always told me that. [Laughing]

Krista: Did she used to say you were a glutton for punishment?

Jodi: [Laughing] Yes!

Krista: Okay. And you are. It's okay, me too. But you always know you're alive.

Jodi: Yeah.

Krista: *"Thank you for the birthday wishes."* Do you realize that your sister doesn't acknowledge your mom's birthday like you do?

Jodi: My oldest sister?
Krista: I don't know; the serious one.
Jodi: Yeah, I can understand that.
Krista: It's like, in her mind, "there's no point because it's like she's not here." And she says, *"How interesting is it that the one I struggled with the most is the one who loves me the most?"* And you do; and you know that, don't you?
Jodi: [Crying] Yeah.
Krista: And she said that's because you learned to appreciate her.
Jodi: Yes. Yes.
Krista: That's what she wanted more than anything, was just this appreciation and this respect. And she's going to have to work on sending you that man. And I love the way she does things. [Interrupted by doing a very strange pointing & snapping thing with my hand] I don't know what the heck I'm doing here with my hand!
Jodi: [Laughing] That's the point, snap. She always did the point, snap.
Krista: That's really strange. Did you use to need to borrow money from her sometimes?
Jodi: She used to just give me money, but it would be at a time where I really needed money. I would never ask for it.
Krista: But what I'm saying is, it would be like, *"Okay, here, let's do this"* and she would just pen you a check or whatever.
Jodi: Yes.
Krista: You're going to love this, Jodi! She says, *"Do we need to get your finances straight?"*
Jodi: Yes! [Laughing]
Krista: *"Well, why didn't you ask?"* You never had to ask; she just knew what you were going through, and she would offer.
Jodi: [Crying] Yes.
Krista: And did she always tell you it was a loan, but never made you pay it back? Or how did that work? Because it's like a loan, but it wasn't really a loan.
Jodi: Yeah, it was just, "What do you need?" And I would always say that I would pay her back, but it never happened.
Krista: Okay. *"And your tab's getting pretty high. But would you like some help with that?"* And it's funny because even though there's no physical in Spirit, she's showing me the pen and the checkbook, and she says, *"How much do you need?"*

Jodi: [Crying and laughing] Just to get by? Or to take care of everything?
Krista: *"How much do you need?"* [In a very firm voice] Oh my God! That was her! [Jodi laughing in amazement]
Jodi: $25,000 would take care of everything.
Krista: *"You want to be more realistic?"* [Looking over the top of invisible glasses, as I hold an invisible pen & checkbook] This is funny!
Jodi: [Still laughing] $1,000.
Krista: I have never had anyone in Spirit offer money! And I know it's funny and deeply hilarious. But when I walk away, I'm going to be going, "Whoa! This should probably go in the book!" But I have to tell you, Jodi, you *are* going to get it. She's not kidding around. And she said, *"You can call it pennies from heaven if you want. Call it what you like; you're going to get it!"* And it's funny that you laugh and everything, but she is just dead serious! That was her thing, wasn't it, dead serious?
Jodi: Yeah.
Krista: Okay, so how freaking cool was that? Could she hang out with my mom? My mom would have me washing her car to earn it! So it's done. You're going to get it. So whatever you need, whatever you're going to spend it on, she wants you to go ahead and get that prepared, because the money is going to be there. *"There you go . . . and Merry Christmas!"*
Jodi: Did she just say, "Merry Christmas?"
Krista: Yes. *"Merry Christmas."* Why did I say Merry Christmas in June?
Jodi: Because that's her favorite holiday. She usually gave the most amazing gifts! She could pick the perfect gift for the perfect person every time! I mean she just really didn't do money as a gift.
Krista: Okay. So, it was just that "wow" thing?
Jodi: Mmm-hmm.
Krista: Okay, so what's next?
Jodi: [Laughing] What else do I need?
Krista: You want the decent man? Or do you want the job?
Jodi: [Laughing] I want both.
Krista: Which do you want first? Oh, God, I know what you want. How about we just work out the job?
Jodi: Yeah.

How Much Money Do You Need?

Krista: *"If we work out the job, then the money takes care of itself. Then when the money takes care of itself, then we'll work on the man, and I don't have to give you more money."*

Jodi: Right. Yeah. [Laughing]

Krista: *"Are you willing to do what it takes?"*

Jodi: Yes.

Krista: *"Are you going to play by the rules?"*

Jodi: [Laughing] That's probably where my biggest challenges are, is playing by *their* rules.

Krista: As much as you wanted to grow up fast, and she wanted to hold you back from that, she is saying, *"It's time to grow up, and to be willing to play by the rules."* This is a serious conversation here, okay?

Jodi: Yeah.

Krista: *"If you're willing to do it, then the job is yours. When you do what they want you to do, the job is yours. If they say 'jump,' you jump; if they say 'walk,' you walk. If you're willing to do it, the job is yours"*

Jodi: Okay.

Krista: And she's not fond of the shoes, by the way. What's with the shoes that she wouldn't like?

Jodi: [Laughing] I don't know; she started it! Maybe the fact that I wear high heels all the time; but she started it.

Krista: She said hers weren't that high.

Jodi: No, but she started it.

Krista: Okay, I'm just telling you what she said. Hers weren't that high.

Jodi: [Laughing] Nope.

Krista: It will kill your back. She went, *"No, not thrilled with the shoes, but whatever, it's okay."*

Krista: You do have a job coming. I feel like it's this job (the one her mom is promising), but you definitely have a job coming. It requires you to be more structured and to try to fit somewhat into someone else's box, which I know sucks!

Jodi: Yeah.

Krista: Do you work out of your house now?

Jodi: No, but I work in a very unstructured environment.

Krista: Right. You can come and go as you please, which is why you're here in the middle of the afternoon. [Laughing]
Jodi: [Laughing] Mmm-hmm.
Krista: So you know that you're going to need to eat a little sh*t?
Jodi: Mmm-hmm.
Krista: Okay, so, the money is yours. So, wherever it's going to go, get it prepared, because it's coming. And have you talked to Jim recently?
Jodi: Mmm-hmm.
Krista: Okay. *"And why did you do that?"*
[Jodi laughs]
Krista: Not me, not me. This is your mom talking.
Jodi: Apparently, because I'm not ready to let go. I'm ready, but I'm not ready; then I'm ready, but I'm not ready.
Krista: And you just need something else to hold on to.
Jodi: Right.
Krista: And is that where this other guy comes in?
Jodi: Mmm-hmm.
Krista: It's funny because the image I get is like how Tarzan swung to the tree, and he always reached another vine before he let go of the first one. And it's like, once he was firmly on the vine, he could let that first one go. [Laughing]
Jodi: [Laughing] Yes, that makes sense.
Krista: I feel like you're really coming to terms, though, with Jim.
Jodi: Mmm-hmm.
Krista: And you're recognizing things, but I do have to tell you he honestly does love you. And I know that you know it in your heart.
Jodi: I do, yeah. I do.
Krista: Your mom said, *"She needs a stronger man than him anyway."*
Jodi: Yeah.
Krista: Was your dad a strong man, emotionally strong?
Jodi: Emotionally strong, yeah. I wasn't really close to my dad until after my mom died, so there is a lot that I don't know about him personally.
Krista: Your dad was frightening before your mom died, wasn't he? And he was kind of standoffish.

How Much Money Do You Need?

Jodi: I was scared of him! He was not around a lot because he worked out of town when I was a teenager. So, it was me and mom. My older three sisters were married and on their own, and it was just me and mom, and he was away working. So yeah, he scared me because usually when he was home; it was more discipline than communication.
Krista: And the roles have switched, haven't they? And now you are the parent?
Jodi: Mmm-hmm. Mmm-hmm.
Krista: Is he staying with someone? Because I don't feel like he's on his own.
Jodi: He has a wife, yeah. And is mom okay with that?
Krista: Yes.
Jodi: Because that happened very, very quickly.
Krista: She is okay with it. She takes care of him, and he will widow her; and you know that already.
Jodi: Yeah. He's considerably older than she is, like fifteen or eighteen years, something like that.
Krista: And it is a good place for now, a good place for them. She says, *"You're an awesome mom . . . and that's what really counts. It doesn't matter who you were yesterday, it's who you are today."* That's important. She would like to hug you. Did she not hug you enough? She just said she didn't hug you enough.
Jodi: [Crying] Yeah. It was usually hellos and goodbyes, but that was about the extent of it, and certainly not when I was little or in all those horrible teenage years. [Laughing]
Krista: Okay. Any last things you would like to say to her?
Jodi: [Crying] That I love her, and she, too, is a wonderful mom.
Krista: *"I didn't always know that, but I tried. I love you."*

In summary: Jodi needed the $1,000 to use as a down payment for her daughter orthodontics. Exactly two days later, her daughter called her and asked for the phone number of the Orthodontist. When Jodi questioned her as to why she needed it, Lydia said that her boyfriend's mother made the offer to pay the down payment.

Also, Jodi began a beautiful new relationship with a wonderful man named Mike within one week of this reading. They are still together today, after a year and a half. And remember when Jodi's mom asked about the job? Well, Jodi landed a fabulous new job in her same field, just four months after the date of this reading!

You just can't make this stuff up!

Chapter 18
Bippity-Boppity-Boo!

Hannah in her "Angel" dress, doing what she loved best . . . Twirling!

Do you remember Shanda, from the Geneser family reading? Remember how little Hannah stole our hearts and touched our lives so much with her warm, joyous and jovial personality? Well, Hannah has blessed us once again in this reading just a few months later. Since I began the "Readings" section of this book with a reading with Hannah, I thought it would be a special treat to end it with Hannah's presence as well.

Krista: I'm going to probably keep my eyes closed for a minute until I can get Hannah fully here.
Shanda: Okay.
Krista: But I do have things to say to you in the meantime. You've come along way, correct?
Shanda: I think so.
Krista: You have. And I know, that you know, that you still have your times and some days are better than others. But are you getting better at expressing this? It's like you can get through a conversation longer.
Shanda: Yes. With being pregnant, the emotions are . . . like some days I can have full blown conversations, talk about her and some days I just . . . I lose it.
Krista: Well, a lot of that is heightened hormones.
Shanda: Yeah.
Krista: It's funny because you know a doctor will tell you that your hormones are never more in balance. And I remember when a doctor told me that, and I thought, "This is how I'm supposed to be?" [Laughing] But I get that you have made a significant amount of progress. Have you started the book yet?
Shanda: No, I have not started the book.
Krista: Okay. Do you know what this book is?
Shanda: I know what I think I want it to be. And I think that it's just about the true emotion – just the things that you go through.
Krista: The steps.
Shanda: Yes! And that what is there is so normal, but also to say, "Here's how it went for me."
Krista: Ah, we are getting a little visitor here [chuckle]
The way I see your book is like that "What to Expect when You're Expecting" book; like that's something everyone needs to read and I see yours as that. But Hannah would like a book about angels. [Laughing]
Shanda: [Laughing] Yes. Yes, it sounds like she does. A children's book, right?

Krista: [Laughing] She would like a children's book, yes. It's about an angel named Hannah.

Shanda: [Laughing] I would love to do that if I can really figure it out. If I know the answers to how you make this better. What is this children's book; not to be so fearful of death because death is not the end? This kind of thing, it's an angel thing?

Krista: [Clapping] Yes. I'm just clapping my hands and this is Hannah doing this. In the book, it's an angel. Her name is Hannah and I feel like she comes and explains to kids; and the idea is letting them know . . . almost like they are going to become angels even though it's not really angels, but that's how she wants it done. [Giggle] And can she be a princess angel? [Laughing]

Shanda: Of course she can! Would I make her anything less than a princess angel? [Laughing] She can definitely be a princess angel.

Krista: [Gasp] What is this sparkly dress?

Shanda: Oh, is it silver?

Krista: Yes. Yes! Is that her dress? Is that like a Halloween thing? Okay, no, that's just her dress.

Shanda: [Crying] Yes! She loved that dress! And that's the dress she was wearing at the viewing. I didn't go to the viewing, but that's what she wore in the viewing, and her sparkly tennis shoes. [Teary laugh]

Krista: She says, *"That's an angel dress, mommy."* [Laughing] And she was a princess in that dress, wasn't she?

Shanda: She was a princess in every dress! Yes she was a princess in that dress.

Krista: Yeah, was she a magical princess in that dress?

Shanda: I don't know. [Laughing] Like I said, she had wands. She was always a princess and she had lots and lots and lots of princess dresses that are still there.

Krista: [Laughing] This is very interesting because I can see it and if I could draw, I would draw this for you; but I can't draw. But you know someone who draws don't you? Who draws? Do you draw? Who draws?

Shanda: Um . . . my dad. My dad draws.

Krista: Your Dad draws. Okay, I feel like if you could see it, you would set it right there in front of you, and you would just write. Did she like pop-up books?

Shanda: Yes! We didn't have a whole lot of them because they got ripped for so many years, but yes. Don't tell me she wants it to be a pop- up book because that's extra hard. [Laughing]

Krista: It's her taking center stage. It's like, "whoop here she is!" She is the star of the show!

Shanda: Yep, that's Hannah!

Krista: And does she have a wand where the head is a star?

Shanda: Yeah.

Krista: Because it's so funny; it's an angel but I swear when I see what she shows me, I want to go, "Bippity-Boppity-Boo!" [Laughing and waving my invisible wand] That's how she's making it look, but this is for children about . . . She (Hannah) interrupts a lot . . .
It's about not being afraid of death, that it is not a scary thing, and that you never die. And what she shows me is like . . . [Hannah shows me the Disney movie, Aladdin] Did she like Aladdin?

Shanda: Yeah. Yes, yes! [Laughing]

Krista: I'm trying to ask her what she is trying to show me, and I see this magic carpet ride. But that's what this is to her. That is what she does all day. She just sort of floats through the atmosphere and it's like a magical ride. [Chuckles] Shanda, I feel that this is important. I know everything is important *to her*, but I feel this would be just as important to children as your other book would be to adults. But I feel like I also have to tell you that it's only the beginning, and I feel like there will be a series. I feel like there are more and it's going to explain . . . [Hannah interrupts]
We are going over all the ways the hair needs to look. Does the hair have to change in every scene? Does she change her hair a lot?

Shanda: [Gasps] She has long hair. We did lots of different hairstyles, I can tell you that.

Krista: [Laughing] I'm just trying to get the gist of what she's trying to show me; and then she just keeps showing me her hair this way, and her hair this way, just all different ways.

Shanda: Were there French braids? Were there braids?

Krista: Yes, there are braids, and there are piggies, and there's something strange that I don't know what the heck it is. And then there this thing on top of her

head and I'm trying to keep focused while she's playing this slideshow for me. [Laughing]
Shanda: She wants different hairstyles in different scenes? That's awesome. Okay, I could see that.
Krista: [Laughing] I guess. It's just her personality. She's just so changing.
Shanda: Yes. Does she want the same outfit in every scene or would she like a different outfit in every scene?
Krista: [Laughing] *"As long as it's shiny. It's got to be shiny."* She likes the shiny.
Shanda: Okay, yes. That silver dress I got her was her Christmas dress and it was silver and flowy and . . .
Krista: Sheen.
Shanda: Sheen, yes! Yeah.
Krista: Okay, almost like a taffeta.
Shanda: Yeah. Yeah.
Krista: That's what she would like to have and . . .
[Sigh, laugh] How much younger is Harper?
Shanda: Than her? Let's see: two years, plus three months.
Krista: Do you recognize, that *"Harper is great and all . . ."* [Chuckle] but were there times that Harper kind of stole the show.
Shanda: Harper or Hannah?
Krista: Yes, Harper. Like your attention had to go to Harper and away from Hannah.
Shanda: Probably a couple of times, but I think Harper really got the shaft. But yes, at night this is specific when I had to rock Harper. Hannah couldn't stand it! She would wait outside the door and she would keep talking to me and she would want to come into the room. That's the only time I really think Harper got all the attention. Hannah got the attention everywhere she went.
Krista: [Laughing] Oh, so it's funny because she loves Harper and it's like, "Harper is a cute novelty. But we are done with her already." You know that kind of thing.
Shanda: Yep. Yep.
Krista: And this is so funny. She tells me, *"Princess Angel Hannah can have someone else in her book, but not on every page."*
Shanda: [Chuckles] Okay. She can have somebody else.

Krista: I think like another little baby or something like a child or sister, but just not on every page.
Shanda: Okay. So, she needs to be the only one on some of the pages.
Krista: She really does. And the sense that I get from this is that there's a child that maybe something happens to or is sick. And before it happens, the angel comes in and tells them, "You're going to come with me on this magic carpet ride." I feel like this is to focus on the transition and not the means by which they crossed. Do you understand that?
Shanda: Yes. Yes, I do.
Krista: It takes this scariness away, because the event is not what's important. The idea that the angel comes and takes them. That is what this is about and it's got to be magical. [Chuckle]
Shanda: Okay, okay. [Laughing]
Krista: It's got to be magical and it is important. I really feel that it's important for kids.
Shanda: Oh, I think you're right.
Krista: Oh, it ain't me. I can't take the credit; it's your little girl.
Shanda: I agree with her; there was no way to . . . Harper was so young when this happened. We didn't really need a book to explain to her, but we talked to her and things like that. But there were books that my parents and my sisters got for their kids and they said they were just not very good.
Krista: This is something, Shanda that will go into places like St Jude's. I mean, it's really important because children who are ill, there's nothing to really explain it, is there? To explain it in a way that doesn't scare the hell out of them?
Shanda: No that's just it. No, there's not.
Krista: I said a bad word.
Shanda: What did you say?
Krista: Hell.
Shanda: [Laughing] Did she get on you about that?
Krista: Yes, she did. I'm sorry. (Speaking to Hannah)
Shanda: It's okay. [Laughing]
She knows what it's like to go to heaven, to transition, to have the angels come, and I don't. And that's why it's kind of an intimidating book for me to write.

Krista: Right. But remember, if you have the angel and you put it in front of you, it will just come to you. And I think it's going to be that she is going to be your pen. I really do. I think it's just going to whoosh . . . and there it is! And it's so interesting because children's books are so simple, and yet they are tough because you have to appeal to a level that you are not accustomed to. But this is something that is probably the most important thing that can be out there because there are sick children all over that don't know what to expect, and there are adults who don't know how to talk to children about it. And whatever exists out there now . . . I don't know what it is, but she is telling me what it's not. It doesn't explain it and it either leaves fear or it leaves a lot of doubt. And remember, she will be the star! Like there is any question whatsoever, right? She will be the star.
Shanda: Of course she will.
Krista: Did you guys recently eat macaroni and cheese?
Shanda: Last night. We eat it all the time – almost every night.
Krista: You know she loves macaroni and cheese, right?
Shanda: Yes.
Krista: Because she is telling me that you make macaroni and cheese.
Shanda: Yeah, yes.
Krista: Well she saw that you ate macaroni and cheese. So she would like to have some macaroni and cheese. [Laughing]
Shanda: Okay, okay. Anytime! [Laughing]
Krista: Was that her favorite food? Or one of them?
Shanda: Yeah. Macaroni, pasta was her favorite food, just pasta of any kind; red sauce, macaroni and cheese, you name it.
Krista: Did she have a stuffed rabbit?
Shanda: Yes, she did have a stuffed rabbit!
Krista: She did have a stuffed rabbit, okay. I see all rabbits as Peter Rabbit. Ok so she did have a stuffed rabbit. Is it the one that stays on her bed? What is it that stays on her bed?
Shanda: Oh, all of her stuffed animals stay on her bed. The rabbit is actually down with her sister now. Her sister has that rabbit. But she was given that rabbit by people that took care of her when she was young. But there are lots of stuffed animals up on her bed still and there might be a rabbit mixed in.

Krista: No, this is the rabbit; this is the right one. Because I was going to ask you if her sister is sleeping with the rabbit now.
Shanda: Yes, yes!
Krista: And she showed me that the animals belong on her bed.
Shanda: Animals definitely; animals go on her bed. But the rabbit is with her sister. Yeah. Is she upset about that?
Krista: No, she said it's okay. [Laughing]
Shanda: Are you sure? Because I can put it back up on the bed.
Krista: No, it's okay. But does the sister throw it down on the floor?
Shanda: Yes. She doesn't like that?
Krista: Okay, that's what she doesn't like, is it being thrown to the floor. But Harper – isn't she like all over the bed? She sleeps like a fish out of water?
Shanda: Yeah, I think she does, yeah.
Krista: It's the being on the floor that she doesn't like. She is very particular.
Shanda: Yes, well I can understand her not wanting her rabbit on the ground. We have a "no touch rule" on a lot of her things upstairs, but that one got through somehow. Well, Harper does get certain things of Hannah's. At first we were so, "No, you can't touch." And then, we were like, "That's just silly." So now we say, "Those are sissy's, but she shares with you." Harper will even say, "This was sissy's, but she's sharing with me."
Krista: That is so adorable. Are they in the same room? No, they _were_ in the same room.
Shanda: They were, yes. They were upstairs together, now one of them is downstairs and hers (Hannah's bed) is upstairs.
Krista: So, recognize that she has been to your house, since you guys have done that. She knows what's going on with her stuff and she knows what you had for dinner last night. That's so funny. [Laughing]
Shanda: Yeah. [Laughing]
Krista: Did she like sherbet? What is the . . . it's like ice cream, but it's not just basic ice cream? What was her favorite ice cream? Because this is like an ice cream treat, but it's not like basic ice cream.
Shanda: Was it like blue and red?
Krista: Yes. It's very colorful; that's why I thought it was sherbet.

Shanda: She always would like it at the lake when the ice cream truck would come around. She would always get the ice cream bar that looked like Dora or Spider Man; that was always colored. They were probably made of sherbet. I have a picture of her with one in her mouth. Yes, that's what she always liked.
Krista: Jamie had a very difficult time talking about this; accepting it, dealing with it, anything. It's just like tunnel vision to anything else but that.
Shanda: Absolutely!
Krista: Is he getting better about that?
Shanda: No, he is actually getting worse, I think.
Krista: Do you have concerns that with this other baby, it might make it worse for him?
Shanda: I have concerns because I don't know how any of us are going to feel. It's hard to know if it's going to get harder because it's going to feel like . . . I know this sounds kind of weird, but it's like a betrayal. It's like a replacement, but, it's not, you know? Obviously, it's not to us, but it's like . . . I don't know. For this baby, I'm going to love it with all my heart, just like I love Hannah and Harper. But I don't want to have resentment that she is here because Hannah is not.
Krista: Okay. Did you guys choose to get pregnant again?
Shanda: We were trying and then we stopped. Then when we weren't trying, I got pregnant.
Krista: And you said, "Oh crap! Maybe this is not a good idea."
Shanda: Right because I had medication [Laughing]
Krista: [Laughing] She talks loud too. She talks loud because she has to be heard.
Shanda: Mmm-hmm. Oh yes.
Krista: Like kind of screechy [Laughing] so that you heard her. You heard her when she said something.
Okay, I'm sorry. [Apologizing to Hannah for calling her loud]
Shanda: [Laughing] But you definitely heard her!
Krista: Okay so do you also recognize that in a very real way, you guys needed this?
Shanda: Yes
Krista: Did you used to tell her that it was adult time to talk?
Shanda: Yes.

Krista: Because that's what she is telling me. She's telling me its adult time so she's going to be quiet now.
Shanda: Oh yes, yes I did.
Krista: Did you and Jamie . . . I feel like everything with Hannah, it pushed you away, brought you together, pushed you away, brought you together.
Shanda: Mmm-hmm.
Krista: The night that I came over there; was that the first time in a very long time that he showed any emotion, was when she touched him through me?
Shanda: Oh yes! He does not show emotion very often.
Krista: Because Hannah felt like that was going to help, so I felt that would be an open door for him and that he needed to keep the momentum going. But he did not do that, did he?
Shanda: No
Krista: Do you recognize at all that Hannah has made it a lot easier for his father to show emotion?
Shanda: Oh, absolutely!
Krista: It really has! It's changed him for the better, in a major way.
Shanda: Yes.
Krista: But Jamie is just like his mother, at this point.
Shanda: Yes. At this point, yes; very much so. And that's why these two do it. [Speaking of the Hannah Geneser Foundation] Dan and I have always had a hard time diving into the foundation because it's hard for us. But that's how they show their emotion; they put everything, heart and Soul into her foundation. Those two do so much! Yes, you are right; they are the same.
Krista: If he doesn't deal with this, he is going to really crash and I think you know that. I feel like having the new baby is going to bring this right back for him. It's almost like going, "Okay, are you ready to feel? Are you ready to feel?" And if he doesn't, it's going to make it so much worse for him. So, I have to give you that I see this. It's almost like he has to be stoic. Have you dreamed of her recently, since I've been in town?
Shanda: Yes! I think it was not last night, but the night before last. And of course, I can't remember it. But I know I did because I woke up and I said, "I dreamed of Hannah!" And it had been a while.

Krista: [Laughing] Yes, it had. Just know that is her. You know that isn't really a dream?
Shanda: Right. It's hard to conceptualize that it is not a dream. That's what I have been told, that it's not a dream; it's a visit.
Krista: Yes, it is. She knew that I was coming here and that I was going to talk with you. And it was interesting because it was Friday night when we were doing the gallery. But you didn't come and before the gallery, she was hanging around.
Shanda: She was?
Krista: Oh, Yeah. I don't know if you were planning on coming and didn't come, and that's when we filled the room with about fifty people. So, I figured she would come visit you because she was here. [Laughing] She likes yanking on your clothes because that's what she did the night I had remembered to email you back.
Shanda: She was pulling on yours?
Krista: Yes. There's another place, there is another wall she is on. What is that? Is it school?
Shanda: I don't think so. No, not school.
Krista: What is it about the school? Her name is not on a wall at school? Was it on a wall at the school after this happened?
Shanda: There was an art show when this happened. They had an art show coming up, a gallery art show and all their best stuff was displayed. And they had a big thing of Hannah there with all her artwork. She was like the main deal.
Krista: Mmm-Hmm, which she needs to be, because she is!
Shanda: Yes, right.
Krista: [Laughing] Always.
Shanda: Right. So yes, it had her picture.
Krista: Did you consider moving, but changed your mind?
Shanda: Yes
Krista: Okay. Are you certain, being where you are is the right thing? Or do you have questions about that?
Shanda: I have questions about that. The reason why was because I was fearful that we have a beautiful upstairs and the baby has to go upstairs, and there is a playroom upstairs. And I don't like it up there because that was her room and her stuff is there. So we're in the process right now of changing it into kind of a

family room, play room. Putting skylights in, so there's more light. We are doing other things, but we can't get ourselves to take her bed down so we just moved it and put it right back up with all her stuffed animals. I can't move her clothes. It's hard. I thought I could do it, but I'm not ready for it I suppose. But that was the fear that this room would always hold so much negative feeling for me and such a heaviness, and I didn't want to be in there.

Krista: But the other part of you doesn't want to give it up.
Shanda: Correct.
Krista: And you found your middle ground with that.
Shanda: I think so. I told my husband I'm throwing caution to the wind after this is all done and it's going to change the way I feel. I just don't know.
Krista: I don't see that you are in a need to move but, you will settle in with it more. Okay?
Shanda: Okay.
Krista: Is there anything you want to say to Hannah? Was it a Mickey Mouse ice cream bar? I just keep seeing these ice cream things. She was a healthy eater, wasn't she? Meaning she had a healthy appetite.
Shanda: She was a good eater. I mean she would eat, and at school sometimes she would eat seconds.
Krista: Is Harper the pickier one?
Shanda: Yes. [Laughing] Yes.
Krista: Do you have a vacation coming up? When is that?
Shanda: Mmm-hmm. June 28th
Krista: Are you going somewhere beachy?
Shanda: Yes!
Krista: [Laughing] It's going to be really good. You're going to need that. It's almost like your big hoorah before the baby.
Shanda: That's it exactly. Yes
Krista: I feel like Harper has or had a love-hate relationship with the water.
Shanda: She loves it. She just took swimming lessons this year. At the beginning of this year, she was just so scared. Now she loves it.
Krista: Okay because I see her and she is in, then she's out. Then she's in, and then she's out.
Shanda: Yeah.

Krista: Hannah is excited! [Clapping hands] When she blew kisses she blew with her palms and not her fingers, right?
Shanda: [Laughing] Is she doing that? [Gasp] Yes! Yes!
Krista: She loves you soooo big! [Arms outstretched & head up]
Shanda: Is she doing that?
Krista: Yes. What is the moon? Does she love you to the moon? Is that what she is saying?
Shanda: [Crying] Yes! She loves me to the moon and back. We always did that before we went to bed.
Krista: *"I'm here mommy! I'm here."* She says don't be sad. That's what she would say. *"Don't be sad, mommy. Why you cry, mommy?"*
Shanda: [Crying] I just miss her so much.
Krista: She misses you, she does. But it's different. She is going to help you tell the story. *"See you later ally gator."* Ally, ally, ally gator? Yeah, see you later ally gator. Who did she call pop-pop?
Shanda: [Laughing, crying] Papa, Jamie's dad.
Krista: Papa, okay. *"Give papa kisses."*

You just can't make this stuff up!

Standing between the Worlds

If you look closely, you can see three orbs in the photograph. The largest is located just above the boy in the hat; the next size down is next to the girl who is holding the two babies, nearly on top of her face; and the tiniest orb of all is directly above the oldest boy's head.

Part III
Wrapping it up:

If, before picking up this book, you had any doubts whatsoever about the ability to effectively communicate with those in Spirit, your doubts should now be completely dispelled. Hopefully, I have answered any questions you may have had about the afterlife between the covers of this book.

It is also my hope that you now have a clear understanding about the responsibilities of a medium, as well as knowing how a reading takes place and what you (as a client) can reasonably expect during your own mediumship reading. If you have never had a reading, but have always wondered about communicating with your loved ones in Spirit, hopefully you will now feel more confident and comfortable in doing so. If you have loved ones in Spirit that you wish to connect with, please find a reputable, professional medium to facilitate that connection for you. This will ensure the best possible outcome for you, thus it will have the highest potential of bringing about the healing, closure, or close, intimate connection that you may be seeking. Please remember that a higher reading cost does not necessarily ensure a better reading, though, as with any professional service, there is a definitive value that goes with the territory.

I hope you have thoroughly enjoyed the communications between those in Spirit and their families. It was originally my intention to end this book right here. However, I have added these next few chapters to give you the best possible experience, leaving you with very few – if any – questions about Spirit communications.

Included in the final segment of this book is a very special chapter, dedicated to the families of the children whose readings I'm sure you've enjoyed. I'm quite certain that you will be deeply touched by the genuine, heartfelt letters of appreciation from the mothers who have so graciously volunteered to tell their story. The intention of those letters was not to build a larger client-base for myself, but to show you, the reader how deeply healing and transformational this work really is and how much it means to so many!

Chapter 19
Keeping the Relationship Alive

*P*ERHAPS THE BIGGEST STRUGGLE I HAVE SEEN in my work as a medium is the ability for others to keep the relationship alive after their loved ones have passed. As insensitive as this may sound, I honestly was not aware that so many people struggled so much with this. Looking at it now, it seems kind of silly that I would just expect others to know what I know. It was not until it came up in a conversation I had with my friend, Lenore that I became aware of how many people honestly do not know that they can indeed have a relationship with their departed loved ones . . . right now, today.

Lenore had asked me, "Why is it that I am almost continually aware of my father's presence, but almost never of my mother's?" I asked her to explain to me her relationship with her father, and then also, her relationship with her mother. I could clearly see by her dialogue that she still held onto a great deal of pain with her mother's passing. She was still relating to her mother's *death*, while she was easily and beautifully basking in her father's *life*. Do you see the difference here? Please go back and reread that last statement, as it holds the key to the level of understanding we **must achieve** in order to *continue* a relationship with our loved ones. I gave Lenore a brief exercise she could try at home. She agreed to try it, we said our goodbyes, and hung up the phone.

The next day, I received a very excited telephone call from Lenore. Being the softer, subtler energy that she is, I had never really experienced that type of excitement coming from her, so I was naturally intrigued and very curious to find out what had brought this on. She was beaming with joy and excitement as she shared with me her experience from the night before. Not only had she learned to initiate contact with mother on her own, but she had also learned how to stay present in a relationship with her . . . *today*!

This was not only a fantastic experience for her, but it also revealed a hidden revelation for me that would be the precipice for this entire chapter. For, it was during this exercise that Lenore could finally see that as a medium, I simply do not have the ability to see things the way that my clients or most other "normal" people see them. In other words, I don't have the ability to un-know what I already know. For me, I have always known that our loved ones are right here with us, and that because they are with us and because we can contact them at will, we have the ability to *continue* a relationship with them. With this brought to my awareness, I now feel that I have the duty to at least attempt to help my readers with this task.

I received an email from Lenore later that day. She was writing to tell me that following our conversation, she began to hear wind chimes in the breeze around her, which is her signal for her mother's presence. She then began getting information that she was to sit down and write. I would like to share that writing with you now, as an opening for this chapter, as it is so very fitting. There was no title on this piece, but I have named it for its use in this book:

The Other Side

You will not find me in your memories of the past
You will not find me at my grave or my urn – only my name
You will not find me within your feelings of sadness or anger
or judgment or abandonment or regret
You will not find me as you relive my last days
in my physical body or the moment that I left
I am HERE – A living Spirit . . . with you . . . in the NOW!
It is only the limitations of your physical eyes that cannot see
But you can feel my presence . . . and feel my love
I send you signs and thoughts and inspirations and messages
Feel me by your side as you greet the sunrise of a new day
Feel me by your side as you count the stars in the night sky
I can meet you anywhere in your dreams, if you prefer
I am watching and will be with you at all of your life's celebrations

*I will bring to you encouragement and support
during your difficult lessons
I can feel your heart and your love
I love your smile and enjoy your laughter
Let me help you solve your life's problems
My advice to you is live life fully
Savor every day
Love well
Laugh often
And when your lessons are complete
and it is your time to return home
You will see me clearly and I will walk with you . . .
As you cross to the Other Side*

Lenore Hamill

Now, as promised, here is the exercise I gave to Lenore. Try it for yourself and open the lines of communication between you and your loved ones. They are just as eager to have a relationship with you as you are with them. I will give this to you in an easy-to-follow, step-by-step formula. There are some things that you should know to begin the process of "opening up" to those in Spirit.

♥ **Shut down the sadness.**

Lenore's poem touches on this when she says, *"You will not find me within your feelings of sadness or anger or judgment or abandonment or regret. You will not find me as you relive my last days in my physical body or the moment that I left."*

It is those thoughts that lead to feelings of heartbreak and despair. Any time that we are in a saddened emotional state, we are in a lower vibrational frequency . . . and we will *never* be able to reach such a high, ethereal energy from that place! Remember that those who are in the spiritual realm are not only *at*, but they literally *are* a very high vibrational frequency. They cannot stoop or sink all the way down to reach us; we must raise our vibration (our mood) to meet them somewhere in the middle. This is the exact reason why so many of our loved ones will only visit us in our sleep shortly after their passing. While we are awake, we are in a place of despair and sadness; though when we sleep, we let that part of ourselves go . . . we shut down the thinking part of our brain, which in turn, stifles the heavy emotions.

♥ **Keep it real.**

So many of us like to idolize and idealize our loved ones after their passing; it's human nature to want to remember the best in them. However, it is this same process that *keeps them from us.* They do not have deep regrets about us and they do not see us as perfect people who have never done anything wrong. They see us just exactly as we are; it is only those of us who are still in mourning that cannot face the truth that everyone has their flaws and faults . . . and that it's perfectly okay. Could you imagine trying to have an honest, solid relationship with another person (in the physical), if you idolize them and refuse to see them for whom they really are? By not seeing them through eyes of truth, you are also not accepting them, therefore, your whole relationship would be based on a lie . . . and it would be unsustainable. That's one of the reasons why it's easy for a medium to connect with your loved ones; they are not personally involved, therefore they do not have low vibrational thoughts and feelings about them. There is more about this in the final chapter of this book, "The Cycle of Life."

This reminds me of a quote I heard from a minister many years ago: *"God is more motivated by inspiration, than desperation."* That is very suitable to what we've just talked about. The word inspiration means to be "in Spirit" or "with Spirit." When we are of low vibrational frequency, we will not be able to attract that which is of high frequency. Now that you have a basic understanding of the energy of those in Spirit, I will now share with you the steps to initiating a connection to them.

1. **Open the lines of communication.**

    Just as in life, the very first step to establishing any kind of relationship is opening the lines of communication. This sounds like a no-brainer, I know, but you would be surprised at the number of people who are not aware of this all-important step. Your loved ones are almost always trying to commune with you, but they cannot get through if you have built a stone wall around yourself.

So how do we open communications between ourselves and those in Spirit? To begin with, we must turn off or otherwise disconnect ourselves from the thought activity of the brain. I know this sounds treacherously difficult, and for many, it can be. However, like anything in life, with enough practice, we can master it. Turning off the chatter in the brain is just a matter of erasing thought. Get into a quiet space in your mind, a space where you are not allowing your brain to wander aimlessly from one thought to another. A tool that worked well for me when I was learning to meditate many years ago was to envision an exit door in my brain. Whenever any thought would creep into my mind, I would envision it leaving through the exit door. It took a lot of practice and during my learning curve; many useless thoughts were shoved out into the ethers, never to be seen again.

Another good tool for raising your vibration, shutting down thought activity, as well as "summoning" or tuning in to feel those in Spirit is music. I have always considered music to be "The Language of the Soul." Many years ago I wrote a very upbeat pop-rock style song in remembrance of a young lady who was a long-time family friend. I always use this song to "call in" Spirit when conducting group readings, galleries, or other public mediumship events and demonstrations.

2. **See them, and then see *into* them.**
When trying to connect with your loved one, see their face in your mind's eye. Remember to see them as holy and whole, not ill or injured. Hold that vision clearly, sharpening your focus along the way, until you have a crystal clear vision of them. This can also be done by staring at their picture, though you must be even more careful to not allow disparaging emotions to come into play. Once your vision of them is solidly focused (whether it's a mental or literal picture), look deeply into their eyes. Remember: "The eyes are the window to the Soul."

3. **Bring in the love.**
Now that you have peered into the Soul of the person you are connecting with, you must raise your vibrational frequency even higher to bring yourself

into closer vibrational alignment with them. There are only two feelings that I know of that can raise your vibration that high, that quickly: Love and Gratitude.

Feel the love that you have for that person. Feel it; experience it; expand it . . . until it is larger than life! Feel it as if it is a liquid that is filling you up; feel it penetrating your very being and exuding from the pores of your skin! The very energy of God is Love, and once you are experiencing love as a verb *and* a noun, you are raising your own vibration exponentially! A word of caution: Be careful not to slip into missing this person, as that will shut you down in a heartbeat!

At this point, it is very important to feel and express gratitude. Be grateful for their presence in your life. Be grateful for the time you had with them when they were "here." Be grateful for their presence in your life *NOW!*

4. **Feel their presence.**
Once you have successfully gone through the previous steps of initiating communication with your loved ones, now you will likely be feeling them all around you. Even if you do not recognize what you are feeling, you may still notice some sort of shift in the atmosphere around you. You may notice that the temperature has gotten cooler or warmer. Maybe the hairs on your body will begin to stand up. Or perhaps you will feel like there's a subtle breeze in the space around you.

5. **Ask for a sign.**
This is a perfect time to ask your loved ones to engage in a two-way conversation with you. Ask them to do something for you; touch your arm, or hand, or cheek; ask to smell them; ask them to show you something (in your mind's eye). When asking for an image, such as their favorite memory or their favorite thing in life, pay close attention to the thoughts and/or images that immediately come into your mind. Another thing that I have instructed clients to do is to ask them for guidance in your life. Here are a few examples:
- ♥ "Mom, you know that I'm struggling with whether or not I should move. Please bring me a white feather if I should move or a brown feather if I should wait."

- ♥ "Grandpa, you know that I have a new job offer on the table. Please help me figure this out. Send me pennies (with significant dates) if I should take it or nickels if I should not."
- ♥ "Dad, I really love knowing that you're here with me. Please just keep me mindful of your presence, and do so in a way that I will recognize."

The reason I am instructing you to ask for "yes" signs as well as "no" signs is that you will be encouraging dialogue no matter what. If you only asked for a white feather, and you received no feather at all, you may begin to doubt that you are actually communicating with your loved one, when in fact, the answer may simply be "no."

6. Gratitude, gratitude, gratitude.
Now that you have experienced an open dialogue with your loved one, express your gratitude for their presence. Anchor your relationship with your loved ones in gratitude. It is the key that opens many of life's doors.

Once you have successfully made that initial contact with your loved one, you only need to repeat it in order to keep it going. Before long, you should be able to connect with them simply by envisioning their face. They are probably not the ones who need help doing this; usually it is we who need the help. When you feel them – or think that maybe you feel them – bring them in! Talk to them . . . aloud. Ask questions and pay attention to the first thought that comes to you. When we have a thought that is placed there by ourselves, by our own brain, it is usually constructed, meaning that it is built-upon, and not a whole and complete thought that swoops into our mind all at once. When we have the all-at-once, complete "thoughts" that just happen to answer a question that we've been entertaining, that is not our brain putting them there. That is telepathic communication from the world of Spirit.

There are many people who will consult with a medium and call that brief interaction a "relationship" with their loved ones. At the risk of putting myself out of work, it's important that you know – that everyone knows – that we *really can* enjoy a present relationship with those from our past. Personally, I would be thrilled to be the go-to medium for every person on the planet. But I would better serve the world if I taught you to *continue* your relationship with your loved ones and I simply stepped in on occasion.

On a personal note, I also have loved ones in Spirit, and I choose to maintain a relationship with a few of them. Even so, I still have my annual reading with a medium friend of mine. After all, even a dentist has a dentist. Having a trusted professional we can consult with prevents us from distorting information we may be given from our loved ones in Spirit, and that helps us to navigate life with more assurance and confidence, thus leading a more fulfilling and harmonious life. An ethical medium will not create a sense of dependency in her clients, but will ensure them of their loved one's continuous presence, thus encouraging a truly sacred relationship between them and their loved ones.

Chapter 20
The Results

We were so blessed to have Hannah's mother write the Forward for this book; what an amazing gift she has given us all with her words of love, hope, and encouragement! After reading Shanda's words – so raw, so true and touching, I was inclined to ask Misty and Zachary's mothers to also make a contribution to this book as well; now we are triply-blessed! On the pages that follow, are the genuine, heartfelt expressions of Treva Ambrose and Kimberly Nelms. It is my sincere hope that the stories all of these mothers have chosen to share with you will touch your heart and bring tears of love and compassion to your eyes, just as they have mine. Only through hope, can one open their heart enough to allow others to see through the pain and into the Spirit that *IS LOVE*. Please know that every time you read these stories, you are connecting with the Spirit of these children and painting them back to life. In the words of Shanda Boone:

"We, the living survivors of death, are not forsaken."

Standing between the Worlds

Treva Ambrose

On June 18th 2012, the day after Father's Day, we received news that no parent ever wants to hear. On our front porch stood a highway patrol officer telling us that our baby girl had been killed in a horrible car crash! She was only fifteen years old.

My name is Treva Ambrose, and my husband's name is Michael. Our daughter, Misty was the light of our lives. She had a huge heart and spent her time on this earth making everyone around her laugh. Every morning before school, Misty made it a point to come find me and let me know that she was leaving, and to tell me that she loved me. I cherish those times, now more than ever and there's is nothing that I would not give to hear those words from her lips again! We sought help, grasping at anything to teach us to cope with losing our baby. We went to therapy and talked with friends and family. I prayed, I cried, and I felt like I would die. We begged God to help us. And Naturally, We asked "Why us?! Why Misty?!"

Sixteen days after Misty's death, her dog, Daisy ran to the front door and started barking like there was someone outside. We went to the door and looked outside – nothing. Nobody was walking by; there were no cars or animals. We decided to snap some pictures with the flash to see if there was something we couldn't see in the dark. I told my eldest daughter, Jamie "I just don't think I'm going to make it through this" and then I prayed aloud "God, PLEASE just let me see her one more time!" In the photographs, I could see what looked like white smoke in the images, and three weeks later, when I got the photos developed, I sat and stared at them in awe. I showed my husband, brother and kids. We all saw the same thing – MISTY! In that picture was our beautiful daughter smiling, her hair was parted the way she always wore it, she was wearing purple (her favorite color) and she had the most beautiful wings you could ever imagine! I knew in that moment that Misty was with me that night, and that God was listening to me! I was given a gift that could never be replaced!

We first met Krista a few months after Misty's death, when our neighbor recommended her to us. She came to our home, knowing nothing about our family, who had passed, who we wanted to contact, or the nature of the passing; and she

The Results

sat and talked with us. She told us that Misty was there, and that she would never leave us. It was good news - but naturally, we were skeptical . . . until she told us so many things that she couldn't possibly have known! Krista asked us if Misty had been struggling shortly before her passing. We said, "No," but Krista said, "It feels like she was, because she keeps saying, *'I'm free now.'*" After the reading, I showed Krista a poem that Misty had written, and it made me think, "Maybe she *was* struggling a bit." Her poem talked about freedom from a world of hate and anger. Misty was wise beyond her years!

After our reading, we had no doubt that Misty was there with us that day, and that she always had been! We also knew in that moment that she always would be. Krista told us that we would start noticing things, signs. When we go to her crash site now – we FEEL her presence!! We KNOW she's there with us! All of our pictures are purple and have beautiful orbs in them! We have several videos taken at our home and the orbs are present in the videos, too! As plain as day, Misty is there, dancing with us, adding her light to the pictures and videos. She's showing her happiness in everything around us.

Misty's Uncle Darrel and I were outside one day, and in all of my years I had never seen a more gorgeous sky! It was bright orange! We looked at Misty's window . . . and there we saw her! My God! She was as beautiful as ever, her gorgeous hair blowing in the wind. My husband even got to see her that day! It was amazing. Just beautiful! Even in death, Misty has found a way to make us smile, to remind us of her sparkly nature.

There was a morning that I was lying in bed, and I felt the presence of someone lying behind me. I assumed it was my husband, but he wasn't even home. I could feel the weight of someone behind me, but there was no physical body in bed with me. It was Misty proving to me that she is always there with me.

I truly believe that Krista opened those lines of communication for us. She gave us hope when we had none! After being empty for so long, I now have something to look forward to! I am learning to find joy in things again - and that is something I thought could never happen. For so long, I was really focused on the details of that crash and very angry and bitter about the nature of Misty's passing, the lack of remorse from the driver, and the injustice in the court system. It took me a very long time, but one day, when speaking with Krista, she read to me, Misty's poem that was mentioned in the reading, and she said, "Treva, Misty does not want this for you! She does not want you to become the hate and anger she talks about in this poem. She wants for you, 'never ending skies of blue, where you can skip and laugh and play,' because that's where she is right now. She is free, but your anger and un-forgiveness have made you a prisoner. You need to find that place of hope and joy and love, because that's where Misty is and that's what she would want for you." It was very tough to hear those words, but I knew that she was right. I was constantly focused on her death, and not on her life. And the biggest thing Misty has been showing us in her Spirit photos is that she is ALIVE . . . now more than ever, and in a way that we could only hope to be!

It has been sixteen months since we lost Misty and I can honestly tell you that this is the hardest thing that we have ever had to face! At first, every day was a struggle; but now, we are learning – even if only a little bit – how to get by, how to live. The biggest thing that has helped us is knowing, beyond a shadow of a doubt, that Misty is here with us all the time; she is helping to ease our pain little-by-little and dry our tears, one-by-one. I still have rough days, but I feel at peace knowing that my daughter's Spirit is VERY MUCH ALIVE! She is showing us every day that she is there, in her own way . . . the only way she knows how. Misty is there for us always . . . just as she promised in the reading.

I am truly grateful for Krista. She gave us a gift beyond comparison. She showed us that we could communicate with Misty, but more importantly, she showed us that we can carry on, and that the love we share with Misty will be the crutch that holds us up in times of struggle. The bond that my daughter and I have is truly unbreakable . . . not even death can change that! I found this little quote, and it reminds me so much of Misty. The last line rings true now, more than it ever has:

"I believe that imagination is stronger than knowledge. That myth is more potent than history. That dreams are more powerful than facts. That hope always triumphs over experience. That laughter is the only cure for grief. And I believe that love is stronger than death."

Thank you, Krista, for showing us the way.

The Results

Treva has graciously allowed me to share with you, the readers, the poem that means so much to her, that has helped tremendously in softening her heart and opening her up to the healing that Misty so wanted for her mom!

My World

When I am alone
When no one can hear me
Laugh, cry, and scream
I'm in a world of peace
A world where only the sun shines forever
A world where I can be a kid forever
The clouds white and puffy
The sky never ending and blue
That's where I meet you
I see your face, I smile
I awake and I cry
You leave and I scream
You take my hand into
A world so perfect, so joyful
We run, skip, laugh, and play
Until it's time to snap back
Into reality where there is
So much hate and anger
Among the world
I can't wait to go back to bed

Misty Ambrose

Kimberly Nelms

On February 26, 2012, I received a heart-wrenching phone call from a girlfriend letting me know that her son, Alex had taken his life the same way that Zachary had taken his only two years earlier. My heart sank knowing the pain that lied ahead for her. I felt the need to help her through the nightmare she was facing, but this wasn't a dream at all; it was very real. I needed to be strong for her, but all the pain of losing Zachary came bouncing back like a ball that was out of control, as I ran to my friend's side on that horrific day!

The very next day, I called Krista to let her know about my friend and her son. I knew that Krista could hear the pain in my voice as I told her all about what had happened. Krista asked me when I was going back to see my friend and she said that she would like to see me before I went, and she said that she could help me, if I wanted her to. I told Krista I was going to see my friend that afternoon and that I did want her help.

As I drove to meet with Krista, I pushed a button to play a CD that was created for Zachary's funeral/celebration of life. The last song I heard as I pulled into Krista's driveway was, "With Arms Wide Open," by Creed.

Krista performed an emotional healing technique called "Havening," which was to help with reducing and/or overcoming traumatic or stressful memories. There were a couple of events that were brought out that I had been storing and suppressing, along with the pain of losing Zachary. During the Havening, I felt very safe, like when I was a child, feeling my mother's touch, soothing away the pain.

After the Havening, Krista also performed a cleansing on me. This cleansing made me feel like there was so much love in the room; this love surrounded me, like the sunshine on an unclouded day. All I could feel was LOVE and PEACE; this was a peacefulness that I couldn't remember ever feeling before! I felt like angels were gathering all around me, and a sensation like someone had lifted me from the table that I was lying on. I can remember seeing a bright light through the lids of my closed eyes, and just knowing that I was loved deeper than I could have ever imagined! It felt like the smile on my face was a permanent fixture that could not ever be removed.

The Results

Krista thanked me and I couldn't understand why she was thanking me, I was the one who should be thanking her! I felt that such a heaviness had been lifted from my chest and Krista was my angel on earth on this day. Krista told me that while performing the cleansing, she had seen something that she had never seen before. My thoughts were "how cool!" For some time, I had not felt worthy of God's love; but not on this day! I thanked Krista for being there and helping me in my time of need. I felt ready to be the rock that my friend was going to need in dealing with the loss of her son . . . and I was.

On the day of Alex's funeral/celebration of life, I decorated the main room for my friend and her son, just like I had decorated the Funeral Home for Zachary just months before. I wanted everything to be just perfect! I was able to do just that, right down to the wonderful smelling flower that she wore, pinned to the front of her dress.

Alex left a note behind for his loved ones and in it was a request for a specific song to be played in his remembrance: (Leave Out All the Rest, by Linkin Park). I think this is very important and so did he for everyone to remember to let go of the hurt and anger inside that you're feeling from the loss of your loved one. Focus on the life that you had together here on earth, knowing they are always with us and will be until we are reunited one glorious day. I know that my son Zachary will push his way to the front of the line when we are reunited. But until this day comes, he will continue to communicate with me and show his love every chance he can. Our bond and love will stay strong, even though he is gone from me in the physical.

(Chorus)
When my time comes, forget the wrong that I've done
Help me to leave behind some reasons to be missed
Don't resent me, and when you're feeling empty
Keep me in your memory
Leave out all the rest
Leave out all the rest

After my readings with Krista I feel that I am more at peace with the loss of my son. It doesn't mean that I miss him any less, because I miss him every day. But I know that he will always be with me and I have a very special angel looking over me and he shows his love for me every chance he gets! I also know it's okay to be angry at someone for taking their own life; or remembering the bad, funny, kind, quirky, loving times you spent together. So many times I have only wanted to remember the good times, and blocking out the bad. I didn't want to remember the arguments, or that he wasn't the perfect child. But I know now that it's okay; and I will kick Zachary's butt when I get there . . . right after I hug his neck and rejoice from all the love that will be surrounding us!

I want to say Thank You to a very special person/friend in my life, had it not been for her, I'm not sure where I would be today.

Lots of love, Krista Kaine. Lots of love.

Kimberly Nelms

⁓

We are now near the end. You have been intimately privy to the private Spirit communications within this book, and you have peered into – and likely even cried as you have felt the pain and grief, the love, hope, and healing that a mother experiences after the loss of a child.

Perhaps now we can answer the questions that Shanda Boone posed in the Forward of this book: "How does a parent survive the death of their child? How is it possible to get out of bed and face the day in the absence of your child's smiling face and heartwarming laughter? Where do you find comfort when you can no longer hold them in your arms and wrap your love around them?"

Do you know the one, single answer that encompasses all of these questions? I do. And I know that Shanda answered this for all of us towards the end of her statement:

The Results

"We, the living survivors of death, are not forsaken."

From this knowledge, we come to a place of . . . HOPE

Having
Optimism (for)
Peace (and)
Enlightenment

Chapter 21
The Cycle of Life

*I*N CLOSING OUT THIS BOOK, I WOULD like to share something very personal with you, the reader. Hopefully, this will solidify many things for you. This book was extremely late going to press and I've had many people eagerly awaiting its release. But if there is one thing I have learned, it is that timing is everything . . . and we are not as in charge as we may think. It is no coincidence that the final chapter of this book – which seemed like a complete afterthought, should be written during this particular period of time.

Today is September 23, 2013, and the twelve-year anniversary of my mother's passing. This day means so much to all who love her; some will visit her grave, some will cry an ocean of mournful tears in memory of her illness and subsequent passing, some will attend church services and bring her picture to the altar, and some (myself included) will bake her favorite cake in honor of loving what she loved. However, regardless of how other family members and loved ones choose to think about and honor this day, because of what I do and what I know as Truth, I see things so much differently than those around me. The short and to-the-point statement about how I truly feel is oftentimes seen as near-blasphemy by some. So, I will preface my statement with the explanation of *why* I feel the way I do . . . and then, I will expand on it for you.

My mother is a larger-than-life presence, who made absolutely no excuses to anyone. (Notice I used the word "is.") She is a strong, stern, confident, charismatic, funny, passionate, loyal, determined, and very opinionated woman who knew no middle-ground in anything at all. Things were black or white, right or wrong, good or bad. You either loved her, or loathed her; there was not much in-between. Myself? I loved her *always* . . . and I loathed her from time to time. Realize that my sporadic feelings of anger and resentment did not detract whatsoever from my love for my mom. I believe that if we were all completely honest with ourselves regarding the truth of our relationships with those who have passed (with the exceptions of small children), each one of us would probably make similar proclamations, just as we do with people who are still in the physical. Think about it: There are some people we love, some we loathe, and others who elicit no feelings from us whatsoever.

But something happens to those of us still in the physical, when a loved one dies. Something inside of us often has this overwhelming desire to idealize and idolize the person who has passed. For some, this may be a mechanism to guard ourselves against guilt or regret; for others, it may be something altogether different. Yet the Truth of it is probably more simple and natural than any of us may realize. Perhaps it is the evidence of a realization that the little (or even the not-so-little) things that irritated, or even enraged us in life were really not that important after all. Perhaps it is simply the Spirit within us calming and taming the ego that is also a part of us; maybe it's our ability to see someone through the eyes of God. As beautiful and satiating as that thought is, it is not until we can bring ourselves *past* the point of idealization and idolization that we can fully heal from our own sense of loss. It's about getting to – and *accepting* the Truth.

The Truth is that we are all multidimensional beings, whose mission it is to identify more with the Spirit that we truly are, than with the ego that we *think* we are. And as we are on this journey to self-realization and self-actuation, we find a middle-ground; a place where we can see and know and accept that the Spirit in the person who has passed was flawless perfection, while the personality of the person was not always the easiest thing to deal with. We then surrender any negative thoughts or feelings about the person in realization that it is not important *today*. Once we reach that point with those in Spirit, we can then spread that out amongst those around us in the physical world. We can love the person, without judging the personality.

So, yes, my mother had the ability to shred you to pieces with her sarcasm and sharp tongue, as well as the ability to put you back together again with just one smile, one hug. I miss my mother and nothing would bring me greater joy than hearing her laughter, smelling her skin, seeing her face, or even having her hang the phone up on me out of anger and frustration! (Those who know me can understand her frustration.) But I can now love and accept *all* of her – the good, the bad, and the ugly . . . and I can see perfection in all of it. Being a medium allows me to hear her laughter, smell her skin, see her face, and yes, even hear her correct me from time-to-time. But I am here to tell you that you can do this too! You *can* establish a new connection with your loved ones in Spirit, by seeing them in this exact same way. When we leave our bodies, we are One with Source – One with Truth. If you want to connect with Truth, you have to come *from a place of Truth*.

Without diminishing my eternal love and respect for my mom, I can see the intrinsic value that her departure has created in my life, and because of that, I am grateful. Are you shocked by this statement? Can you now see why I felt the need to preface it for you? This is not to say that I am happy she's no longer with us in the way that we've always known her; it is simply finding the good within the bad. I would love nothing more than to have her back here, in the physical! However, I am extremely grateful for the way that her death has contributed to my life. This does not mean that I do not love or miss my mom; in fact, I can honestly say that I love her in a whole new, and much purer way than ever before! You see, every experience that we have makes a positive contribution to our lives, whether we realize it or not. I would dare to say that the harder the experience, the more value it will bring.

Why am I grateful for my mom's passing? *Because* you are reading this book. *Because* Shanda Boone has found hope and healing from our interactions with her precious little girl. *Because* Treva Ambrose is learning to live from a place of forgiveness, and she's learning to experience a whole new level of relationship with her beautiful daughter, Misty. *Because* I spend every single day of my life doing what I love and being whom I was made to be.

Remember Chapter One, where I spoke about how I had turned away from my gifts and tried to squash any attempts that Spirit had to bring me into fullness? *None* of this – *none* of who I Am, *none* of what I do, *none* of the healing that I have contributed to in the hundreds or even thousands of lives would have been possible had my mother not ascended to Spirit. I would *still* be right where I was all those years ago; I would *still* be struggling to find where I fit in, to learn who I Am . . . and to even find a way to love myself. That is the most tremendous gift of all! *Because* of my mother's passing – *because* she came to me in my slumber to lend her seal of approval for this work, I have known peace and I have helped to facilitate that same peace in the hearts and minds of countless others.

My mom was my rock . . . always! She was the first person I'd turn to in times of joy and in times of hardship. That part, I miss greatly. However, while she was here in the physical, she also enabled me to live far beneath my potential; she enabled me to stay in neutral, to stay "stuck." She used to tell me regularly that I needed to learn to stand on my own two feet, instead of standing on hers. One thing she said so often in my adult life will stay me forever and I use these words to propel me towards the direction of my dreams: "Krista, I'm not going to be here forever, you know. You've got to learn these things sometime. You've got to learn to manage your own life."

She was absolutely right! And because I leaned so hard on her, when she passed away, I was stifled – completely immobilized! I honestly did not know *how* to live without her. I did not know *how* to be my own woman, to solve my own problems, or to achieve my own goals. There is no doubt in my mind that if she had never gotten sick, if she were still right here today (in the physical), I would be the same ineffective person I had always been. Now that she is in Spirit, I can see quite clearly that at times – many times, I'm sure; I was a complete drain to her. Although she never uttered those words, I'm quite certain that she felt the effects of it. I am very proud to say that I am now living my own life, solving my own problems, and achieving my own goals. This very book is evidence of that . . . and I am so incredibly grateful to my mother and to you, the reader for helping to bring this to life.

How about some more evidence of gratitude for my mother's contribution? My mom was an integral part in raising my first two kids, and my third child, up until he was he was nine-years-old, for that's when she passed. Had my mother not passed away when she did, my last two children would have been raised under the same religious and dogmatic beliefs and constraints with which my other kids were raised. They would have been taught things that I have always known in my heart were untrue; they would have heard and learned things that may have very well caused the same inner conflict that I had experienced most of my life. Because my mom is no longer in the physical, I have been able to ingrain into my two youngest kids that they are living, breathing, walking, talking expressions of God; that they are perfect, loving beings with unlimited blessings and potential as their inherent birthright. I have also been afforded the ability to teach these things to my three older children, whom are now adults, though it is much more difficult to impress upon the mind of an adult than it is a child. My eldest son still believes – to some capacity – in Satan and hell and judgment. He still believes that he is a limited being who is not fully and easily afforded all that his heart desires. Although his awareness has come a long way since I came out of my "spiritual closet," you still cannot un-ring a bell.

As a closing statement, I would like to share with you a short analogy told by an amazing and inspiring teacher, John F. DeMartini. This is such a beautiful analogy that I think it well deserves to be the last thing you read as you close the covers of this book. Although I do not remember his story word-for-word, it had such a deep impact on the way that I think, that I have referred to it mentally every time something or someone has left my life. I even read it at my uncle's funeral many years ago and my cousin was very touched by these words:

The people in our lives are like the leaves of a tree.
They serve to protect us and to add beauty
and texture to our lives.
The more leaves you have, the more beautiful
and bountiful you appear;
the more enriched your life becomes.
And when it is time for us to grow,
the people will fall away,
just as the leaves will fall from a tree.
Though they do not ever really leave us,
for just like a tree whose leaves have fallen away,
they serve nourish the soil in which we are grown.
This is The Cycle of Life.

About the Author

In addition to being an Author and a nationally known Psychic Medium, Krista Kaine is also a Metaphysical Teacher and Public Speaker, as well as an Ordained Minister and Life Coach who works with her clients in the capacity of Personal Empowerment & Development, and Relationship Coaching/Counseling, from a spiritual perspective.

Krista's work takes her throughout the United States, conducting platform message services, private readings, workshops, public speaking events, and leading church services for New Thought churches and Spiritual centers. Krista refers to her work as:

"All branches of the same tree, whose body is rooted in Spirituality."

To inquire about scheduling services with Krista, you may contact her at: Kristakaine@ymail.com

For more information, more great products, or to learn more about Krista's work, please visit her website: www.KristaKaine.com

Made in the USA
Charleston, SC
19 July 2014